Prime Ministers Of Britain

508

Prime Ministers Of Britain

Eileen Hellicar

With drawings by
Shirley Curzon

DAVID & CHARLES
Newton Abbot   London   North Pomfret (Vt)   Vancouver

FOR MY MOTHER

British Library Cataloguing in Publication Data

Hellicar, Eileen
  Prime Ministers of Britain.
  1. Prime ministers – Great Britain – Biography
  I. Title
941.07'092'2   DA28.4

ISBN 0–7153–7486–9

Library of Congress Catalog Card Number: 77–85014

© 1978 Eileen Hellicar

Set by Trade Linotype Limited, Birmingham
and printed in Great Britain by
Redwood Burn Limited, Trowbridge & Esher
for David & Charles (Publishers) Limited
Brunel House Newton Abbot Devon

Published in the United States of America
by David & Charles Inc
North Pomfret Vermont 05053 USA

Published in Canada
by Douglas David & Charles Limited
1875 Welch Street North Vancouver BC

Contents

Acknowledgements

I should like to thank Caroline and David Blomfield, Janet Brown, and Maurice T. Ragsdale for their professional help, Shirley Curzon for drawing the portraits, Audrey Tapley for typing the manuscript and my mother, Daisy Hellicar, for compiling the index and constantly encouraging me while I was writing the book.

The small figures throughout the text refer to historical events, which are explained in more detail on pages 143–8.

Introduction

'Read no history: nothing but biography, for that is life without theory.'   (Disraeli)

Since Walpole established the position of prime minister two and a half centuries ago, forty-eight men have brought their individual characteristics to the office. Some, like Walpole, were corrupt, for that was the way of politics in the eighteenth century, others were incredibly honest. Some were warm and lovable, others cold and distant. Many adjectives describe them —brilliant and witty, dour and pessimistic, obstinate, ineffectual —and in this book their characteristics are described so that we can compare one against the other, and see how they shaped the office of premier.

Walpole assumed the premiership because George I could not speak English and therefore could not understand parliamentary meetings. Kings and queens were originally the 'prime' ministers, choosing their own royal servants and directing the government as they thought fit, but gradually the influence of the monarch waned and, from the time of Queen Victoria, the prime minister has been chosen by parliamentary majority and not by the monarch.

The personality of the prime minister also led, indirectly, to the formation of political parties. The Whigs and Tories of the seventeenth and eighteenth centuries were not parties as we know them today, but were originally supporters or opponents of James II's right to the throne. The supporters, led by the Earl of Danby, called their opponents Whiggamores (Scottish drovers), for they were mostly Scottish Presbyterians. The opponents, led by the Earl of Shaftesbury, called the supporters Tories, an Irish name for a band of outlaws opposed to protestantism. And so the derogatory names of Whig and Tory stuck. In the ensuing battle for parliamentary authority, the Whigs and Tories, who were then composed of disagreeing factions, gradually formed parties of their own, until they eventually became the Conservative, Labour and Liberal parties that we know today.

The prime minister now has complete authority—he chooses and dismisses his own ministers and he alone can dissolve parliament. The premiership is the most important position in the country and the aim of this book is to describe the men who have shaped the destiny of Britain. It is not a history book but rather a collection of short biographies of the nation's leaders through the centuries, from Walpole to Callaghan. The size obviously limits its content, but I have tried to give a general picture of each premier according to his importance, and to give the facts as I found them and not an opinion. I have also endeavoured to set out the material in easy form for quick reference and at the same time to make it interesting to readers and to lead them on to further reading.

When I told Janet Brown, whose professional help I have acknowledged, that I intended to write the book, she wrote to me: 'It sounds a lovely book—nobody knows better than a history student how dull some of these "Prime Minister" books are! A readable survey will be very welcome, if not by the academics, then certainly by their students who welcome any short cut.'

I sincerely hope that that short cut has been provided.

Eileen Hellicar
Mitcham, 1977

Sir Robert Walpole (1st Earl of Orford)

Born 26 August 1676
Married (1) Catherine Shorter
(3 sons, 2 daughters) (2) Maria
Skerritt (2 daughters before
marriage)
Ministry 1721–42 (Whig) –
Kings George I and II
Died 18 March 1745. Buried at
Houghton, Norfolk

Sir Robert Walpole, Britain's first prime minister, was a fat, coarse-mannered man, with a vulgar belly-laugh. He 'always talked bawdy', he claimed, 'because in that all men can join'. He was lecherous, enjoyed drinking large quantities of alcohol, and had a great weakness for eating chocolate. He also liked to lead the hunt across his lands in Norfolk, and it is said that he always looked at the hunting news before attending to his official correspondence. Yet, despite his wayward habits, his brilliant mind brought him to the highest office in the land.

It was quite fortuitous that he went into politics at all. The third son of a family of nineteen, he was destined for the Church, as younger sons were in those days. He had been educated at Eton and Cambridge for this purpose, but both his elder brothers died and Robert inherited the family estate. He was twenty-four. As a rich country squire, he was able to follow his ambition to go into politics.

He entered the House of Commons as Whig member for Castle Rising, Norfolk, in 1701. At that time, the Tories were in the majority, but the Whigs gradually gained power. He was an excellent speaker, and soon made his way in the party, becoming a member of the Admiralty Board, Secretary at War and, in 1709, Treasurer of the Navy. Then the Tories regained power and tried to destroy the Whigs, accusing Walpole of receiving an illegal payment for a supply of forage to Scotland while he was Secretary at War. He was tried by the House of Commons, found guilty and, in 1712, expelled from the House and imprisoned in the Tower. He was freed after six months when Parliament ended its session, and was returned for King's

Lynn in the election that followed. The Whigs again took power when George I became King in 1714 and Walpole was made Paymaster General and leader of the House of Commons. A year later he became First Lord of the Treasury and Chancellor of the Exchequer. Then George I, who could not speak English, gave up attending meetings of the House, as he was bored by not understanding the proceedings, and Walpole became chairman and Whig leader.

Confident of their supremacy, the Whigs quarrelled among themselves and forced Lord Townshend, Walpole's brother-in-law, out of office. Walpole also resigned. The King was horrified and refused to accept his seals of office when he handed them back. But Walpole insisted, so did the King, and ten times in all the seals were proffered and refused. Eventually Walpole won, and he remained out of office for three years. By 1720 the Whigs had united their party and Walpole returned to office, but as Paymaster General again, not to the cabinet.

Then came the South Sea Bubble.[1] Walpole had shares in the South Sea Company, but had astutely sold his stock after making 1,000 per cent profit, before the bubble burst in 1721. Thousands of people lost their money and there was a public outcry. The Government was now in a shaky position: one minister was expelled, another committed suicide, and it seemed that only Walpole, with his financial acumen, could save the situation. On 3 April 1721, the King once again made him First Lord of the Treasury and Chancellor of the Exchequer, and immediately Walpole began to restore public credit. He was now accepted as Britain's 'prime' minister, and remained so from that day until 2 February 1742—the longest reigning premier in history.

Walpole wanted peace—for his party and for his country. He squashed the Jacobites by deviously banishing their chief supporter, Francis Atterbury, Bishop of Rochester. Then he got rid of John Carteret, a friend of the King and thus a menace to Walpole, by sending him to Ireland as Lord Lieutenant. He abolished tariff duty on many articles and instituted a sinking fund[2] to help reduce the national debt. Wages were maintained and prices stabilised by improved industry and shipping.

Walpole, favourite of the King, was favourite of the people. He loved this power, and to stay in office he used every trick of corruption and bribery he could muster. *'Quieta non movere'* was his maxim—'let sleeping dogs lie'. Stepping over the sleeping dogs, shutting up the barking ones, Walpole went from strength to strength. He was the King's man, and in 1725 he was knighted.

When George I died in 1727, Walpole informed the estranged Prince of Wales of his father's death. The Prince, who was not on speaking terms with his father, had his own Court and his own Treasurer, Sir Spencer Compton, and resented Walpole, his father's favourite minister, so he told him to take his orders from Sir Spencer.

Walpole, sure now that his demise had come, humbled himself before Compton, cunningly offering any assistance to the putative prime minister. Sir Spencer prevailed upon Walpole to write the new King's first speech to his privy council. Walpole drafted the speech, adding praise for his own government, which Sir Spencer copied out and presented to the King, who accepted it.

The exultant Compton began to act with condescension towards Walpole and other members of the Government ignored him. Then at the court of St James's the question of the Queen's jointure and the King's grant was being discussed. Compton proposed £60,000 per annum for the Queen but Walpole, seeing his chance, suggested that he ask Parliament to grant £100,000. This was agreed. When Compton suggested that the grant to George II should be the same as his father's, £700,000, Walpole proposed that it be increased to £800,000. This, too, was accepted. Walpole had triumphed. Compton's time had not arrived, and the delighted King confirmed Walpole in his office.

He soon established good relations with the new King, who presented him with No. 10 Downing Street,[3] and he had a firm friend and ally in Queen Caroline. Indeed, he knew that he needed Caroline to make the King take his advice. George II was a bumptious little man with a very bad temper, but he was completely under Caroline's thumb. A popular rhyme was sung about him:

> You may strut dapper George,
> But 'twill all be in vain;
> We know 'tis Queen Caroline,
> Not you, that reign.

It was a sad day for Walpole when she died in 1737.

In 1739, against his wish, Walpole was forced to declare the War of Jenkins' Ear[4] on Spain, but he was no war minister, and he mishandled the whole affair. In 1740 the Commons moved a motion that the King be petitioned to remove him from office and although the motion was defeated, Walpole's position was shaken. In the following year's general election a number of anti-Walpole members were returned and were intent on getting rid of him. (They called themselves 'Patriots', Walpole scornfully called them 'Boys', and they eventually became known as 'Boy Patriots'.[5]) Walpole's defeat came on 2 February 1742 because of a rigged election at Chippenham. Bribery and corruption had been used more than usual and Walpole had no choice but to resign.

A few days later he was created Earl of Orford, given a pension of £4,000 a year and took his seat in the House of Lords. He was still extremely influential and was highly amused at the power-struggle taking place in the House of Commons. His health began to deteriorate and he made his last public appearance in the Lords on 29 February 1744. He died on 18 March 1745 and is buried at Houghton.

Walpole had been a great man and a great prime minister despite the bribery and corruption which was part and parcel of British politics in the eighteenth century.

Spencer Compton (Earl of Wilmington)

Born 1673
Unmarried
Ministry 1742–3 (Whig) –
King George II
Died 26 July 1743. Buried at
Compton Wynyates

Spencer Compton was a shadowy figure—in fact very little has been recorded about him—and his ministry was something of an anticlimax after the sparkling era of his predecessor, Robert Walpole.

During the first part of Robert Walpole's long ministry, Compton was Speaker of the House of Commons and Paymaster General. He was also treasurer to the Prince of Wales, who had his own court as he was not on speaking terms with his father. So, when George I died in 1727, Compton hoped to become prime minister, since he was favourite of the new King, George II. Nothing came of his expectations because the wily Walpole inveigled his way back into office (see p 11).

Walpole, safely reinstated as prime minister, considered it unfair to ask Compton to continue to serve under him as Speaker—he probably wanted him out of the way, anyway. So Compton was made Baron Wilmington and elevated to the House of Lords. Two years later he became an earl. Still he longed to be prime minister. He had come very close to it and he knew who was responsible for his missed opportunity. He now secretly loathed Walpole, and voted against him at every opportunity. Then in 1742 Walpole resigned, and the King asked Compton to form a government.

After more than forty years in Parliament he had achieved his ambition, but he was prime minister in name only. The butt of satirists and cartoonists, he was an indecisive man, with little talent and no strength as a leader. John Carteret, as Secretary of State, led the administration—while Walpole sat smugly in the House of Lords.

The Earl of Wilmington formed his administration in February 1742 and was prime minister for seventeen months. Towards the end of the year failing health forced him to leave London and he died on 2 July 1743.

During his tenure of office, Britain entered the War of the Austrian Succession[6] against France. George II led his troops into battle at Dettingen and narrowly escaped death, but little else happened. He is barely remembered, but even so he had been a loyal, hard-working politician.

Henry Pelham

Born 1695 or 1696
Married Lady Catherine
Manners (2 sons, 6 daughters)
Ministry 1743–54 (Whig) –
King George II
Died 6 March 1754. Buried at
Laughton, Sussex

Henry Pelham was considered to be the real successor to Sir Robert Walpole—Earl Wilmington having been merely a stopgap prime minister while the Whigs sorted out their differences of opinion.

The second son of Baron Pelham, he was educated at Westminster School and Hart Hall, Oxford. In 1717 he entered the House of Commons as MP for Seaford and four years later he became one of the Lords of the Treasury in Walpole's government. He was very attached to Walpole and, according to the Whig writer, Lord Hervey, 'was more personally beloved by him than any man in England'. He quickly climbed the political ladder and with his brother Thomas, Duke of Newcastle, who was to succeed him as prime minister, played his part in retaining Whig supremacy. When Wilmington died in 1743, Pelham became prime minister. After a year in office, he reconstructed his administration on what is known as the 'broad bottom' basis (the original coalition)—this included some Tories as well as Whigs.

The King was not happy with the Pelham administration, wanting instead his friend, John Carteret, in office. So Pelham resigned, but was out of office for only two days as Carteret could not form an administration since both the Commons and the City financiers made it plain that they did not want him. Unless Pelham was premier, no financial aid would be granted for the War of the Austrian Succession.[6] Consequently, Pelham returned to office.

He was an honest, if timid, politician and with the support of his brother, as Secretary of State, his ministry was a strong one. His interests were mainly domestic and he was responsible for a number of social reforms. He had no serious rivals to worry about, but he did have to be careful of the King's whims.

Eager to end the war, he accepted the French proposals for peace, which led to the Treaty of Aix-la-Chapelle on 7 October 1748. He then concentrated on reducing national expenditure and by the winter of 1749 had secured the reduction of the interest on the national debt from 4 to 3 per cent. Among the acts he passed were the act to reform the calendar and the act for the naturalisation of Jews, but the latter he had to repeal the following year because of its unpopularity.

Pelham's parliamentary conduct was approved of by the King, and when he died suddenly of erysipelas on 6 March 1754, George II was very distressed. 'Now I shall have no more peace', he said.

Duke of Newcastle (Thomas Pelham)

Born 21 July 1693
Married Lady Henrietta
Godolphin (no children)
Ministry 1754–6; 1757–62
(Whig) – Kings George II and
III
Died 17 November 1768. Buried
at Laughton, Sussex

The Duke of Newcastle was a fretful, fussy man, full of fears and jealousy. He was desperate for power, but his talents were not as great as his ambitions, and he was lampooned and satirised by all the leading writers of his day. The only good thing they said about him was that he was uncorrupt.

The elder son of Baron Pelham, he inherited the estates of his maternal uncle, the Duke of Newcastle, when he was eighteen and was created Duke of Newcastle in 1715. The death of his younger brother, Henry Pelham, was a great blow to him, but while he was publicly grieving for his brother he was privately

15

making sure he would step into his shoes as prime minister. This he did, in April 1754, one month after Henry's death.

He formed his administration mainly from Whig peers. The Elder Pitt was not promoted from Paymaster General as he had hoped, having held the post for ten years, and this so incensed Pitt that he bitterly attacked Newcastle and his ministry. Newcastle eventually dismissed him, but out of office he was even more troublesome. Newcastle's task was not easy. Charles James Fox, his Secretary of State, resigned; the Seven Years' War,[7] which had now broken out in Europe, was shaping badly, and Admiral Byng had failed to save Minorca. Newcastle was subjected to parliamentary and public outcry until, unable to withstand the pressures against him, he resigned on 26 October 1756.

He was succeeded by the Duke of Devonshire, with Pitt as Secretary of State. But Devonshire was unable to form an administration capable of winning the war. Meantime, Newcastle had retired to his country home, Claremont, in Esher, Surrey, to live the life of a country gentleman, but he soon tired of country pursuits. Devonshire, too, was growing tired of his unsought role of prime minister, and informed the King that he wished to retire. So in July 1757, Newcastle returned as prime minister and reluctantly formed his coalition with Pitt.

Pitt, now Secretary of State under Newcastle, was responsible for foreign affairs and the direction of the war. Although Newcastle was prime minister and responsible for the Treasury, Pitt was the voice and strength behind him. Together they managed a successful administration. Four great victories were won—Quiberon, Lagos, Louisburg and Quebec—but the war was costing a great deal of money and Newcastle wanted to end it. Already he had increased various taxes and customs and excise duties to pay for it and, fearing public reaction to further increased taxation, he borrowed heavily from the City; consequently the national debt increased.

In October 1760 George II died. George III, who disliked Newcastle, was anxious to remove him and the other Whigs inherited from his grandfather. So he appointed his favourite, the Earl of Bute, as Pitt's fellow Secretary of State. Together the King and Bute played on the rivalry and jealousy between Newcastle and Pitt. Pitt resigned from office in October 1761 and Newcastle, acknowledging defeat, resigned on 26 May 1762.

He was almost in his seventieth year and had been in parliament for forty-five years. He became Lord Privy Seal in Lord Rockingham's administration in 1765 until August 1766. He gradually became senile and died on 17 November 1768.

Duke of Devonshire (William Cavendish)

Born 1720
Married Charlotte Boyle,
Baroness Clifford (2 sons, 2
daughters)
Ministry 1756–7 (Whig) –
King George II
Died 3 October 1764

The Duke of Devonshire was a reluctant premier, not wanting the office at all. When he was asked to head an administration, he accepted only on condition that the King would allow him to retire if he did not like the appointment. He was a very rich man, happily married, with a high place in society; he belonged to the country's leading Whig family, the Cavendishes, and had no need for political ambition.

He was thirty-six when he became prime minister and at the time was the youngest person in Parliament. With the Elder Pitt as Secretary of State, Devonshire was virtually 'prime minister under Pitt'. He disliked every minute of his period in office and resigned after seven months, in July 1757. Although he was undistinguished and ineffectual, he was honest and uncorrupt, and the King was reluctant to release him from office.

With the accession of George III, Devonshire fell out of favour both at court and with the King's favourite, Lord Bute. The King and Tory Bute were determined to break Whig supremacy and to humble the powerful Whigs, particularly the Dukes of Devonshire and Grafton. The King removed Devonshire's name from the list of Privy Councillors, and Devonshire resigned his Lord Lieutenancy of Derbyshire, taking himself completely out of office. In 1764 he became ill and went to Spa in Belgium. He died there of dropsy in October 1764, at the age of 44—making him the shortest lived of all British prime ministers.

Earl of Bute (John Stuart)

Born 25 May 1713
Married Mary Montague (13 children)
Ministry 1762–3 (Tory) – King George III
Died 10 March 1792. Buried at Rothesay

Lord Bute came to power, not through his political expertise, which was virtually non-existent, but simply because he was the King's favourite.

The elder son of the Earl of Bute, he succeeded to the earldom when he was ten years old. Being Scots and distantly connected to the Stuart royal family, he was not over-popular in England. He was an intellectual, vain and aloof, and more interested in botany and zoology than politics.

In 1737 he was elected representative peer for Scotland, and this three-year spell in the House of Lords was his only political experience prior to becoming prime minister. A vote against Walpole's Government prevented him from being elected for a second term, and he returned to Scotland, where he lived the life of a recluse among his flora and fauna.

In 1747, out of touch with life, he returned to England and took a house near Windsor. Then began his fortuitous meteoric rise to fame. He was at Egham Races one day when it began to rain and he was asked to join the party of Frederick, Prince of Wales, as a fourth player at cards. He was invited to spend the night at the Prince's home, and so began his close friendship with the royal family.

When Frederick died in 1751, Bute continued his friendship with the Princess and became mentor to the young Prince, the future George III, who was then thirteen years of age. Bute's influence on the Prince was total and he instilled in him his own principles and political ideals. Bute hated Whig supremacy, hated Hanoverian influence on Britain's foreign policy, and hated Britain's involvement in the Seven Years' War.[7]

When the Prince became king in October 1760 Bute's chance came. He was made Secretary of State with Pitt, who was disliked by both the King and Bute. George III was determined to get rid of his grandfather's Whig ministry and on the resignation of the Duke of Newcastle in 1762, he made Bute his prime minister.

Bute's ministry lasted for just eleven months, but during that time he got rid of Whig supremacy by disposing of the Dukes of Devonshire, Grafton and Newcastle, and the Elder Pitt. He brought the Seven Years' War to an end, and signed the Peace of Paris on 10 February 1763.

Although his ministry was politically successful for the King, it was a personal tragedy for Bute, and no prime minister has been more savagely derided. The fact that he was a Scotsman, Tory and royal favourite were disadvantages enough, but added to these was the general belief that he was the Dowager Princess's lover. Disparaging notices were publicly displayed, and rude remarks expressed in public and private. Eventually Bute, an extremely sensitive man could take no more. He resigned on 8 April 1763. But the King still needed Bute and continued to consult him on every matter for the next few years. Eventually the King's affection waned, and by 1770 Bute had no influence over him at all.

Realising that George III no longer required his services, Bute retired to Luton Hoo, his Bedfordshire home, where he followed his cultural pursuits. But still the country was against him and ribald remarks continued to be bandied about. He died on 10 March 1792.

George Grenville

Born 14 October 1712
Married Elizabeth Wyndham
(4 sons, 5 daughters)
Ministry 1763–5 (Whig) –
King George III
Died 13 November 1770. Buried
at Burnham, Buckinghamshire

Although George Grenville's ministry proved to be the strongest in the troubled early years of George III's reign, he became the first prime minister to be dismissed by the King.

Grenville's public image was that of a cold, argumentative bully. The King found him a bore. Yet he was a happy family man with a devoted wife, who took such an interest in his political career that she kept a diary which for years was thought to have been written by Grenville himself.

Before entering the Commons as MP for Buckingham in 1741, Grenville practised law. He was a professional politician, as few men were in those days, and was successful in parliament. When he became prime minister in 1763 he was also Chancellor of the Exchequer.

His ministry was a strong one, but it was in difficulty from the beginning. Common opinion was that he was prime minister in name only and that the King was still influenced by Lord Bute. When he became king, George's mother and Bute had told him, 'George, be a king and rule.' And George III intended to do this. He did not like Grenville and interfered in the running of Parliament, until the prime minister informed him that he must make his choice—support the existing ministry or form a new one. This caused a political crisis from which Grenville emerged triumphant, with the King assuring him of support.

He was now really prime minister with royal patronage. His experience of parliament and his legal knowledge were to prove invaluable to him. One of his first acts was to order the arrest of John Wilkes, MP for Aylesbury and editor of *The North Briton*, a political weekly newspaper. In issue No. 45 Wilkes had published what Grenville considered a 'seditious libel' concerning the King's speech. Wilkes was arrested on a general warrant and sent to the Tower. One of the greatest parliamentary battles of the eighteenth century ensued. Some said parliamentary privilege rendered Wilkes immune from arrest, while Grenville maintained that such privilege did not cover seditious libel. He sought a vote of confidence in the case, intending to resign if he lost. The result was that he won by an overwhelming majority.

Grenville was now extremely popular both at Court and in Parliament. The King had no quarrel with his parliamentary ability, yet soon Grenville was to offend the King personally. Suspecting that Bute was still the power behind George III, Grenville eventually stated that he would not serve unless his consent was obtained by anyone wishing to approach the King. George was incensed. By April 1765 he suffered the first of his many mental illnesses, and it was proposed that regents be appointed to cover his periods of incapacity. In drawing up the list of regents, Grenville omitted both the King's mother and Lord Bute and when George recovered from his illness and realised Grenville's action, he dismissed him and appointed the Marquis of Rockingham as prime minister.

Grenville continued in politics, but never again held office. In 1769 his wife died and, grieving bitterly for her, he himself died the following year.

Marquis of Rockingham (Charles Watson Wentworth)

Born 13 May 1730
Married Mary Bright (no
children)
Ministry 1765–6; 1782 (Whig) –
King George III
Died 1 July 1782. Buried at
York Minster

When George III dismissed George Grenville from the premiership in 1765 he asked the Marquis of Rockingham to form a ministry. It was a very odd choice as Rockingham was not a brilliant politician. He was inexperienced, no orator and was incapable of making decisions, but he was the only man available for the office. The King intended that Rockingham should be titular head of the Government with the Duke of Cumberland, George's uncle, actually holding the reins of power. But the Duke died three months later, and Rockingham became prime minister.

This was not the first fortuitous act to send Rockingham to the top. His very inheritance was because his four elder brothers all died in childhood—he had become Viscount Higham, Earl of Malton, and then 2nd Marquis of Rockingham, all by the age of twenty.

He was immensely rich and a great gambler. When he left Cambridge he went abroad, like most rich young aristocrats of the time. Whilst in Italy he contracted a strange illness, 'a fatal present from the Princess Villafranca' he described it, which was to undermine his already delicate health for the rest of his life. When he returned to England at the age of twenty-one he took his seat in the House of Lords. He soon became leader of the Whigs and got rid of the corruption fostered by Walpole and others. He was always a staunch Whig, so staunch, in fact, that when he was fifteen he ran away from Westminster school to join the Duke of Cumberland's army against the Young Pretender.

He was an honest man, benevolent and amiable, possessing a calmness and clarity of mind, yet during his ministry he did not win himself a great deal of favour because he ignored the King. Even so, shortlived though it was, his ministry successfully established trade with Russia, modified the cider tax and abolished tyranny at home and abroad. All this Rockingham achieved despite fierce opposition. The Whig Party was splintering and the King was conspiring against him. Gradually Rockingham became disillusioned and the King dismissed him in favour of the Elder Pitt.

Rockingham stayed in opposition for almost twenty years, and declined to form a ministry on Pitt's death in 1778; he also refused a position in Lord North's cabinet. However, he accepted the King's reluctant invitation to form a ministry on Lord

North's death in 1782 and the elder statesman became prime minister for the second time on 27 March 1782.

Rockingham still had little regard for the King and before accepting the premiership, he determined that there should be peace and a cut in public expenditure. During this ministry he secured the legislative independence of Ireland; disenfranchised 60,000 revenue officers; made it unlawful for government contractors to be members of parliament, and disposed of many government sinecures. But he did not live long enough to witness the peace he desired. The Treaty of Versailles, bringing the war with France and Spain to an end, was signed just over six months after his death. He made his last appearance in the House of Lords in June 1782 and died on 1 July.

William Pitt (Earl of Chatham)

Born 15 November 1708
Married Lady Hester Grenville
(3 sons, 2 daughters)
Ministry 1766–8 (Whig) – King
George III
Died 11 May 1778. Buried in
Westminster Abbey

Pitt the Elder was largely responsible for building the British Empire, but the great statesman and man of war was no prime minister. His mental health was not strong enough to take the strain.

When he entered the House of Commons in 1735 as MP for Old Sarum he became one of Lord Cobham's 'Boy Patriots'[5] who were struggling to bring about the downfall of Robert Walpole. Pitt was a brilliant orator and attacked Walpole at every opportunity; he also criticised the King and objected to the British Exchequer paying Hanoverian troops. George II loathed him, but Pitt's popularity in the country was going from strength to strength. While Walpole was appeasing Spain before the War

23

of Jenkins' Ear,[4] Pitt maintained his harangue against the government, declaring that only by fighting could Britain be saved, and believing that it could only be saved by him.

His eloquence in the House was something to be reckoned with. A graceful, commanding figure, with piercing hawk-like eyes, his voice always clear and melodious, sometimes a whisper, sometimes a roar, he spoke to be heard. He could declaim as well as argue, and his invective was chilling and intimidating. He was also a great actor, and was always ready with an apt quotation or crucifying remark.

Pitt's energy was getting him nowhere, and little wonder. His insulting remarks about the King and his ministers kept him firmly on the back benches, and in 1744 he suffered the first of the three mental breakdowns which were to dog his political career. Already he suffered severely from gout, which had incapacitated him both at school and at Oxford, and was to be with him for the rest of his life.

The war with Spain was going badly, and Pitt was furious at the way it was being conducted. Still his ideas were disregarded and still there was no place in the government for him. Soon Britain was at war with France—an action of which Pitt highly approved—since he hated France and regarded her as Britain's natural enemy, a dangerous rival for trade and the empire. Again he disapproved of Britain's war tactics, believing that France should be fought at sea in order to destroy her navy and take possession of her colonies. It was his opinion that Britain could not defeat France on land and was only fighting her in Europe to defend the King's beloved Hanover—that 'despicable electorate' as he regarded it. As defeat followed defeat other members of parliament were soon agreeing with Pitt.

The Duke of Newcastle, now prime minister, considered Pitt, in opposition, to be extremely troublesome and wanted to bring him into his Government. The King was adamant—he would not forgive Pitt. However, the following year, 1745, with the war in Europe still achieving no success, and at home the Jacobites rising again, the Government was in a desperate situation, so Pitt was brought in as Paymaster General. This was not the post he wanted for, as a cabinet member he could no longer criticise the management of the war, and as Paymaster he had no say in its organisation. He longed for promotion, but George II still loathed him, and Pelham and Newcastle feared him. His mental and physical health deteriorated and in 1751 he broke down under the strain and stayed out of office for two years. In 1754, at the age of forty-five, he married Lady Hester Grenville, the thirty-three year old daughter of Lord Cobham of Stowe. She was a kind, gentle woman, and a devoted wife, who nursed him through his illnesses and managed his business and financial affairs.

The following year Pitt returned to Parliament, full of enthusiasm. Pelham was dead, Newcastle was in power and, despite the Peace of Aix-la-Chapelle, war in Europe was once again imminent, and once again the Government was ready to defend the King's beloved Hanover. Pitt made a frenzied attack in the House, cursing the 'despicable electorate', and deploring the hiring of foreign troops. When war began he continued his invective. Newcastle, failing to silence him, dismissed Pitt from office. But nothing could silence Pitt—and he was to be proved right. First Minorca, then Fort Oswego, in America, fell to France. Still Pitt raged on about Britain's inferiority on land; France was threatening her in the West Indies, in India, everywhere. Pitt was again becoming insane and, convinced that only he knew how to conduct the war, he silenced the House with a megalomanic speech. '. . . I am sure that I can save this country, and nobody else can.' Pitt had now exhausted Newcastle, and the Government collapsed. Pitt, at last, was given the chance to prove his words.

In the Duke of Devonshire's administration that followed he became Secretary of State, with responsibility for the direction of the war. He dispensed with all foreign troops and assembled his own British troops; he enlarged the size of the Navy and ordered more ships and he made great plans for attacking the French and promised support to Frederick the Great of Prussia. Then in April 1757, the Devonshire ministry ended and Newcastle returned and formed his coalition with Pitt—Newcastle as First Lord of the Treasury and prime minister, Pitt as Secretary of State. It was a successful administration, both men needing the other's assistance. Pitt's popularity in the country was at its peak at this time.

Now concentrating on the defeat of France, Pitt did not worry about the cost of his brilliant plan of attack as Newcastle did. Pitt did not want victory for victory's sake, for each of his intended conquests had an intrinsic trade value. He had learned as a boy from his grandfather, 'Diamond' Pitt, a colourful adventurer and governor of Madras, that Britain was great because of her trade and trade must be defended. The world's riches were there for the taking if you were willing to fight for them, the old man had told him. Trade and war went together. He took his advice from London's experienced merchants: Britain needed Canada for the fur trade, and the West Indies for sugar. These were men like his old grandfather, and they knew.

So began Pitt's empire building: Clive conquered India, Wolfe drove the French out of Canada and North America; the Army and Navy together saved the West Indies and West Africa, and France was being defeated according to Pitt's strategy. He became the hero of the people and the merchants, but his arrogance and greed for victories which would enhance Britain's trade increased. He now wanted to wage war on Spain. Newcastle was uneasy at the high cost of the war which he had to finance. Pitt had no understanding of monetary matters and it became impossible for Newcastle to work with him.

When George III became King in 1760 he determined to get rid of Pitt, whom he disliked almost as much as his grandfather had. The King at once began negotiating peace with France and ignored Pitt's demands to start war with Spain. Pitt resigned in 1761 on the grounds that his advice had been ignored. His resignation delighted both King and Government, and the following year the Seven Years' War[7] was brought to an end by the Treaty of Paris.[8] Pitt was grieved by this treaty, believing it to be a betrayal of all his beliefs.

Pitt was out of office for the next four years during which time he was mentally and physically ill. His visits to the Commons were infrequent, but he spoke fervently against tyranny and in defence of the British colonists in America, and correctly predicted the events which were to take place in that country. When Rockingham resigned, the King reluctantly asked Pitt to form an administration, giving him freedom to choose his own ministers and to have complete control of home and foreign affairs. Pitt's dream had come true—but what a mess he made of it.

He formed an administration of Whigs and Tories, which did not have the support of the House. He made an error of judgement in appointing the Duke of Grafton First Lord of the Treasury, while he himself took the sinecure of Lord Privy Seal, which carried with it a peerage. He immediately became Earl of Chatham and moved up to the House of Lords. At once he lost the popularity of the people. The great commoner was now no longer one of them. Their loyalty and love turned to derision but Pitt, physically and mentally ill, was too exhausted to accept the clamour of the lower House. In the Lords he engaged in angry clashes with his colleagues, and by October he was exhausted and retired to his home in Bath. Without his leadership, his colleagues acted irresponsibly, particularly regarding relations with America. In 1767, Charles Townshend, the Chancellor of the Exchequer, imposed duties on various commodities imported into America, and thus sowed the seeds of the American War of Independence. Grafton found it difficult to control the administration. He and the King tried to see Pitt, but Pitt could not sustain an audience since he was suffering his third breakdown. He tendered his resignation on 14 October 1768.

Although he never held office again, and despite ill-health, Pitt remained in politics for another ten years. He continued to speak against the coercion of the American colonies, and collapsed in the Lords on 7 April 1778 during a speech opposing American Independence. He died on 11 May 1778.

Duke of Grafton (Augustus Henry Fitzroy)

Born 28 September 1735
Married (1) Anne Liddell (3
sons, 1 daughter) (2) Elizabeth
Wrottesley (5 sons, 8 daughters)
Ministry 1767–70 (Whig) – King
George III
Died 14 March 1811. Buried at
Euston Hall, Suffolk

The Duke of Grafton was a shy sensitive man, who loathed publicity and ceremony, yet he was more publicly berated for his personal conduct than any other eighteenth-century prime minister. He was a great gambler and indiscreet womaniser, which led 'Junius', the anonymous contributor to the *Public Advertiser*, to run a campaign of vilification against him in the form of open letters.

He entered the House of Commons in 1756 as MP for Bury St Edmunds, Suffolk. The following year he became the 3rd Duke of Grafton on the death of his grandfather, his father having died previously, and was elevated to the House of Lords. He was a clever politician and, when the Elder Pitt became prime minister he appointed him First Lord of the Treasury. Grafton had always greatly admired Pitt, but his admiration turned to disgust when Pitt forsook his ministry and refused any consultation with himself or the King. But Pitt was suffering his third mental breakdown and was incapable of administering, or discussing his ministry, so Grafton, loyal to King and country, took over.

It was not long before Grafton had made his first great mistake —flaunting his mistress in public. Grafton, a married man with four children, was associating with a Mrs Horton, known as 'everybody's Mrs Horton' since she associated with many rich and famous men. Grafton had been seen at the opera with her and 'Junius' began his letter-writing. This provoked such a scandal that it appeared that Grafton would be forced to resign. But the following year he was saved for the Duchess of Grafton had taken a lover herself, the Earl of Upper Ossory, and had become pregnant by him. Grafton divorced his wife, but did not marry Mrs Horton. Two months after his divorce, in May 1769, he married Elizabeth Wrottesley, daughter of the Dean of Windsor. He abandoned his immoral way of life, became a Unitarian, and wrote a book on morality aimed at the upper classes.

Happy in his second marriage, tired of Parliament, and sickened by the attacks of 'Junius', Grafton resigned his premiership on 27 January 1770. The King presented the Garter to him, remarking that he had never given it with more pleasure and that it was one of the few he gave unsolicited.

Grafton remained in politics, most of the time as Lord Privy Seal, until the Younger Pitt became prime minister in 1783, when he chose to retire to his home, Euston Hall, Suffolk, to follow his country pursuits and collect rare books. He died on 14 March 1811.

Lord North (Frederick North)

Born 13 April 1732
Married Anne Speke (4 sons, 3 daughters)
Ministry 1770–82 (Tory) – King George III
Died 5 August 1792. Buried at Wroxton, Oxfordshire

Lord North has gone down to posterity as the worst prime minister Britain ever had and the man responsible for America gaining independence from Britain. But all the blame cannot be put on North. George III, an old friend, determined to choose his own ministers, appointed North as head of the administration when the Duke of Grafton resigned and used emotional 'blackmail' to keep him there. North was intensely loyal to the king and the king knew it. North even refused to be known as 'prime minister', claiming that there was no such thing in the constitution, and that all ministers were royal servants, owing their allegiance to the monarch.

North was the eldest son of Lord and Lady Guilford, friends of Frederick, Prince of Wales, and their respective sons, Frederick and George (the future king) became friends.

North entered the House of Commons as Tory MP for Banbury in 1754 and became a junior lord of the Treasury in the Newcastle-Pitt administration in 1759. In Chatham's ministry he became first joint Paymaster-General and later Chancellor of the Exchequer, and he made such an impression that the King recognised his potential as first minister. George III was slyly gathering his own party of 'King's friends', comprising loyal subjects of all parties, and did not find his task difficult, since the Whig Party was fragmented into quarrelsome splinters and the Tories were not strong enough to govern as a single party. North initially refused to lead a party assembled by the king, but George finally persuaded him to accept in January 1770.

North was a lovable, kindly man, with a good sense of humour and a very fine wit. He also had a reputation for falling asleep and snoring in the House. On one occasion, a speaker was tediously tracing the history of shipping from the time of Noah's Ark, and when the sleeping North was inadvertently awakened by his private secretary, Sir Grey Cooper, he asked what era the honourable gentleman had reached. On being told 'we are now in the reign of Queen Elizabeth', North said, 'Dear Sir Grey, why not let me sleep a century or two more?'

However, he was no fool and realised he had undertaken a difficult task. He was aware of both the King's stubbornness and mental condition and did not wish to upset him. On the other hand, George maintained considerable influence over his prime minister by bestowing many favours, including the honour of a knighthood and his appointment as Warden of the Cinque Ports. Although his total annual salary was £12,000, he was still in financial difficulties, and his acceptance of George's offer to clear his debts placed North under an obligation to the King.

The quarrel with the American colonies was still smouldering and many British people, including the King, believed that they should be subject to Britain. After the Boston Tea-party[9] North declared that the quarrel was no longer about taxation but about Britain's authority over America. He was in favour of negotiating a settlement, but the King declared that the matter could only be settled by war. North, reluctant for war, misjudged the situation regarding the numbers of men and ships to fight it and, subsequently, he was blamed for every British loss. The prime minister realised that he could not carry out the King's colonial policy and after General Gates' capitulation at Saratoga in 1777, he pleaded for permission to resign. He begged the King, 'Let me not go to the grave with the guilt of having been the ruin of my king and country'. But George was inflexible, and using North's friendship to keep him in office, said: 'Surely you will not desert me as Grafton did?' As Britain became more deeply entrenched in the war, North's ministers abused him, and Charles James Fox threatened him with impeachment. Still the King would not release him from office. In October 1781, the war was brought to an end by the surrender of General Cornwallis, and when he heard the news, North exclaimed with exultation: 'Oh God! It is all over.' The King finally allowed North to resign in March 1782, telling him: 'Remember, my lord, that it is you who desert *me*, not I *you*.'

Despite the fact that North's health and sight were failing, the following year he became joint Secretary of State with his old enemy, Charles James Fox, in the Duke of Portland's coalition government. The King hated the Whigs, especially Fox, and, regarding North as a traitor, he deprived him of the seals of office on 18 December 1783. North never held office again. He remained in the House of Commons until his father's death in 1790, when he moved to the House of Lords as the Earl of Guilford.

Despite his failure over the American War of Independence, North's twelve-year ministry was not an uneventful one, and among the acts he passed was the Royal Marriage Act (1772).[10]

Five years before his death he became totally blind, but his spirits were kept up by his devoted wife and family. He died of dropsy on 5 August 1792.

Earl of Shelburne (William Petty)

Born 13 May 1737
Married (1) Lady Sophia
Carteret (1 son) (2) Lady Louise
Fitzpatrick (no children)
Ministry 1782–3 (Whig) – King
George III
Died 7 May 1805. Buried at
High Wycombe

The Earl of Shelburne was never liked and never trusted by his political contemporaries. They considered him a double dealer, but really he was far too much of an intellectual for the ordinary person to understand him. He was to be appreciated only after his day, and fifty years after his death Disraeli described him as 'the ablest and most accomplished statesman of the eighteenth century.'

He was the eldest son of the 1st Earl of Shelburne and was educated at an 'ordinary publick school', as he described it, 'in Ireland, and at Christ Church, Oxford. Later he was commissioned in the Foot Guards and after service in France in the

Seven Years' War,[7] was made a colonel and appointed aide-de-camp to George III. During this appointment he met Lord Bute who used him to carry messages to Charles James Fox of the opposition, which gained Shelburne his reputation for double-dealing.

On the death of his father in 1761, he entered the House of Lords. Two years later he quarrelled with Bute and the King, lost his appointment at court and stayed out of politics for three years.

At Bowood Park, his country house near Calne in Wiltshire, he established the 'Bowood Circle', comprising many of his fellow intellectuals and academics. Shelburne believed that the intellectual had a large part to play in politics and he and his coterie pioneered many of the political reformist ideas.

He refused all attempts to persuade him to return to the government until 1766 when the Earl of Chatham (Pitt the Elder), who considered him essential to the Government, offered him the post of Secretary of State. He became 'Chatham's man', but the Duke of Grafton loathed him and was determined to get rid of him.When Chatham resigned, Shelburne knew that he was deprived of his protection, and in 1768 he resigned before Grafton could dismiss him.

Shelburne again stayed out of active politics, and in 1771, griefstricken at the death of his wife, travelled to Europe. When Chatham died in 1778 he returned to become leader of the 'Chatham Whigs' and a member of the opposition during Lord North's long ministry. With his very fine brain and personal charm, he was a politician to be reckoned with, although he was detested and distrusted.

Yet, despite his reputation, George III called upon Shelburne to form a ministry when the Marquis of Rockingham died. Having refused earlier when Lord North resigned, this time he accepted. With the Younger Pitt as his Chancellor of the Exchequer, his ministry was successful, albeit very short. He made peace with America and signed the Treaty of Versailles on 20 January 1783, bringing peace between Britain, France and Spain. He cut public expenditure and rebuilt Britain's trade after the American war. Still he was distrusted. Shelburne, in his turn, distrusted the King, believing that George III was simply using people through selfish motivation. After several defeats in Parliament he was convinced that the King had tricked him into office and on 24 February 1783 he resigned and never held office again. In 1784 he was created Marquis of Lansdowne.

Although he was a Whig, Shelburne stood apart from party politics, his political creed being 'to approve every measure on its own ground free from all connection'. He was the last premier to try to govern without the aid of his party.

After the death in 1789 of his second wife, whom he had married ten years earlier, he spent the rest of his life among his intellectual friends at Bowood and his house in Berkeley Square. He died on 7 May 1805.

Duke of Portland (William Henry Cavendish Bentinck)

Born 14 April 1738
Married Lady Dorothy
Cavendish (4 sons, 1 daughter)
Ministry 1783; 1807–9 (Tory) –
King George III
Died 30 October 1809. Buried
at Bulstrode, Buckinghamshire

Although he became prime minister twice, the Duke of Portland is among the least remembered of British premiers. In both his ministries he was merely a figurehead, the administration being led by his stronger ministers.

When he entered the House of Lords in 1761, Portland was young, immensely rich and of upright character, and was much sought after by the various Whig factions. He became a follower of the Marquis of Rockingham and when Rockingham was dismissed from the premiership by George III, Portland went into opposition against the Duke of Grafton. So violent was his dislike of Grafton that he was suspected of being 'Junius' the anonymous contributor to the *Public Advertiser* (see p 28).

In February 1783, when Lord North and Charles James Fox collaborated and forced the Earl of Shelburne's resignation, Portland became Prime Minister of the coalition, with Fox and

North as Secretaries of State, but the Government collapsed in the following December. He became prime minister again in 1807, at the age of sixty-nine, but this second ministry was no more brilliant than his first. He was old and failing in health and unable to control his quarrelling ministers, two of whom, Lord Castlereagh at the War Office and George Canning at the Foreign Office, fought a duel on Putney Heath in September 1809 and then resigned. Portland, who had suffered a stroke the previous month, resigned also, and retired to Bulstrode where he died on 30 October.

William Pitt (Pitt the Younger)

Born 28 May 1759
Unmarried
Ministry 1783–1801; 1804–6
(Tory) – King George III
Died 23 January 1806. Buried
in Westminster Abbey

Known as Pitt the Younger, to distinguish him from his eminent father, William Pitt was born for Parliament.

The second son of the great Pitt the Elder, Earl of Chatham, William was born during his father's greatest year—1759, the year that Clive won India, Wolfe drove the French out of Canada . . . the year the British Empire began. The boy 'breathed in' politics from his early childhood. At the age of seven, when his father became an earl, he was heard to remark: 'I am glad I'm not the eldest son. I want to speak in Parliament like Papa,' and during his youth he spent many hours in the Houses of Parliament listening to his father, imbibing every word and gesture. Too weak from gout to go to school, he was educated at home and, by the age of eleven, he could translate Latin and Greek classics. By the age of fourteen, his health had improved through a 'diet' of port wine, and he went to Pembroke Hall,

Cambridge, where he took his degree at seventeen. He was a brilliant scholar and had inherited his father's brilliant mind—fortunately without the crippling insanity. After graduating he studied law and was called to the Bar in 1780.

Naturally, William decided to become a politician. He was unsuccessful at his first attempt, when he stood for Cambridge University in 1780, but next year he was returned as member for Appleby and entered Parliament as an heir enters his home. He joined the Chathamites, led by Lord Shelburne, in opposition to Lord North and soon proved himself to be a very fine orator.

When Rockingham took office from Lord North, he offered Pitt the post of Vice-treasurer of Ireland—a minor post, but carrying a salary of £5,000 a year. Pitt refused it, saying that he would never accept a subordinate position, and he got away with the conceit. He already had definite ideas about his career and even at the age of twenty-two he was respected.

In Shelburne's ministry of 1782 he became Chancellor of the Exchequer and Leader of the House. With Pitt at his right hand, Shelburne had no need of Charles James Fox, who had refused to serve under him. This angered Fox who now realised that he had resigned in vain, and thus began a bitter rivalry between Pitt and Fox equalled only by that of Disraeli and Gladstone almost a century later.

When Shelburne resigned the following year, Pitt refused the King's invitation to form a ministry, believing that he was not yet strong enough to stand the opposition of Fox and North. The Duke of Portland then headed the North-Fox coalition, but this ministry collapsed in December of the same year and the King again turned to Pitt. This time he accepted and, at the age of twenty-four, became the youngest prime minister in British history. His opponents, particularly Fox, derided his ministry, positive that it could not last for more than a few weeks. But it survived for seventeen years.

An aloof, individualistic man, caring little for party politics, Pitt was resolute in his ideas and ideals. He was firmly against the quarrel with America, bent on parliamentary reform, union with Ireland, Catholic emancipation,[11] the reorganisation of the East India Company,[12] reducing the national debt, and free trade. With little government experience and weak support in Parliament, he suffered many defeats during his first year as prime minister, but he was not perturbed and the more Fox taunted him, the better he responded. Every cutting thrust from Fox brought a more cutting and wittier one from Pitt. Gradually Pitt's support grew, both in Parliament and in the country, and with his own popularity increasing and Fox's declining rapidly, he dissolved Parliament in 1784.

In the election that followed, in which Pitt again represented Cambridge University, he and his supporters were returned with a huge majority. The King was delighted for he had at last triumphed over the Whigs. With strength behind him and no wife or family to divert him, Pitt could give his undivided attention to his political ideals. He immediately set about reducing the national debt and instituted a sinking fund.[2] In 1784 he passed the India Act establishing dual control of the East India Company. 1785 was not such a successful year as his Reform Bill and Union with Ireland Bill were rejected. In 1788 the slave trade agitation began and Pitt gave his support to his old friend, William Wilberforce, the abolitionist. The King was again mentally ill and Pitt's tasks became more difficult as Fox, in opposition to Pitt, advocated the regency of the Prince of Wales; however, the following year the King recovered. In 1791 Pitt passed the Canada Act, dividing Canada between the French and English. Ireland still concerned him and finally, in 1800, he passed his Act of Union. The following year the King refused to accept Pitt's Emancipation of Catholics Bill, declaring that he had sworn to be loyal to the Church of England and would be breaking his coronation oath if he allowed Catholic emancipation; Pitt resigned in consequence.

Pitt was followed in office by Henry Addington. In 1803 war with France was renewed and Napoleon was planning to invade Britain. Pitt's political skills were required to deal with this crisis, and in 1804 the King asked him to form an administration. Pitt reluctantly accepted—his health was failing and he became more and more addicted to port wine, the medicine of his childhood. He wanted to form an all-party administration, and all parties were willing to serve with him, but the King, old and almost insane, obstinately refused to allow Fox into the Government. With Napoleon still sweeping across Europe and intent on invading Britain, Pitt formed a coalition with Russia, Austria and Sweden against France. Napoleon was finally defeated at the battle of Trafalgar, and at the Lord Mayor's banquet at the Guildhall, Pitt was hailed as the saviour of Europe. His reply, which was to be his last speech, is perhaps the best remembered:

'I return you many thanks for the honour you have done me. But Europe is not to be saved by any single man. England has saved herself by her exertions, and will, as I trust, save Europe by her example.'

The coalition was destroyed, however, when Napoleon defeated the Russian and Austrian emperors at the battle of Austerlitz (1805). It was a mighty blow for Pitt. A man of peace, he was griefstricken, and when he saw a map of Europe after the battle he said, 'Roll up that map. It will not be wanted these ten years', for Europe now belonged to Napoleon.

Pitt was indeed a great prime minister who was totally dedicated to his country. His personal life was rather sad and lonely for he had no wife to comfort him and no close friends to confide in. His sickly childhood had made him shy and withdrawn and his complete political absorption had left him no time for social life. His interests were solitary pursuits such as reading and gardening. He hated field sports and did not gamble. Yet, despite his frugal social life, he was always heavily in debt. When he died at the early age of forty-six on 23 January 1806, the House of Commons voted that £40,000 should be given to meet his creditors.

Henry Addington (Viscount Sidmouth)

Born 30 May 1757
Married (1) Ursula Hammond
(2 sons, 4 daughters) (2) Marion
Scott (no children)
Ministry 1801–4 (Tory) – King
George III
Died 15 February 1844. Buried
at Mortlake, Surrey

Henry Addington, the son of the Elder Pitt's physician, was the first British prime minister to emanate from the bourgeoisie. He was a favourite of the King—an honour indeed, since George III detested the middle classes. Dr. Addington, a specialist in psychological medicine, had also won the favour and confidence of the King when he attended him during a period of insanity.

Since boyhood Addington had been friendly with the Younger Pitt and, in 1784, when Pitt called his first election, he suggested that Addington, who was a lawyer, should enter politics and support him in the House. Addington agreed and, with Pitt's help, he was returned as member for Devizes in Wiltshire. He soon mastered parliamentary procedure and, in 1789, Pitt made him Speaker, an appointment much approved of by the King.

The following year Dr Addington died and Henry came into his inheritance. He was now very rich and bought an estate in Berkshire. Addington's friendship with Pitt became closer and his influence in Parliament increased. Pitt proposed Catholic emancipation[11] in 1801, and although both the King and Addington opposed the idea, they were unable to influence the premier to change his mind. The King then asked Addington to form a ministry and, playing on Addington's loyalty, beseeched him: 'Where am I to turn for support if *you* do not stand by me?' Addington turned to Pitt for advice, but Pitt was as adamant as the King: Addington must accept. Pitt pledged his support and promised to rally the support of his ministers. So, on 14 March 1801, Henry Addington became prime minister and Chancellor of the Exchequer.

Not all of Pitt's supporters rallied round the new prime minister, however, for the more senior ministers were pro-emancipation. Addington nevertheless managed to form an administration which included three future prime ministers—the Duke of Portland, Spencer Perceval and Lord Liverpool. One Tory squire exclaimed: 'Thank God for a government without one of those damned men of genius in it'. The King was grateful for it, too, and expressed his thanks, 'Addington, you have saved the country.'

Despite his popularity with the King, Addington was not popular as prime minister. Known derogatorily as 'The Doctor' he was satirised in the press, became the butt of cartoonists' cruel humour, and was sniggered at by aristocrats who were amused by the middle-class prime minister. But, despite his critics, Addington struggled on. He made peace with France and signed the Treaty of Amiens on 28 March 1802. In his first budget he abolished income tax.

His success in government, however, depended upon the support of Pitt, who was beginning to create difficulties and finally withdrew his support. War clouds were gathering once more in Europe and Addington, realising he could do nothing without Pitt, tried to persuade him to return, but without success. In 1803 war with France erupted again and the following May Napoleon mustered his men at Boulogne ready to invade Britain. Such a crisis was too great for Addington to manage; on 10 May 1804 he resigned and was at once succeeded by Pitt.

Pitt invited Addington back into the Cabinet as Lord President of the Council the following year, 1805, and he was created Viscount Sidmouth. On Pitt's death, Addington became Lord Privy Seal in Lord Grenville's Whig administration, from 1806 to 1807, after which he was out of office until 1812 when he became Home Secretary in Lord Liverpool's ministry. He held this post for ten years, during which time he approved the Peterloo Massacre,[13] introduced the Six Acts,[14] suppressed the working classes and prosecuted trade unionists, setting up a network of spies to trap offenders.

Addington, the middle-class prime minister who entered politics to support the Younger Pitt, held office for thirty years in six administrations. He had both enemies and friends, but he was always courageous and loyal, and did what he considered right for his King and country. After his retirement he took little part in politics and devoted his time to good works. Towards the end of his life he wrote: 'I am not aware of having ever wilfully injured or given pain to any human being.' He died on 15 February 1844.

Lord Grenville (William Wyndham Grenville)

Born 25 October 1759
Married Anne Pitt (no children)
Ministry 1806–7 (Whig) – King
George III
Died 12 January 1834. Buried
at Burnham, Buckinghamshire

Lord Grenville was a cousin of the Younger Pitt, but unlike Pitt he was not a born politician. He was more a literary man— a classical scholar from Eton and Oxford—and possessed a fine collection of books and paintings. However, coming from a successful and dutiful political family, he automatically went into politics.

The son of George Grenville, George III's first Whig prime minister, his public image, like his father's, was that of a cold, unsympathetic, obstinate and often inconsistent man. Nevertheless he was honest, industrious and a master of political law, and quickly climbed the political ladder.

Three weeks after Pitt's death, in February 1806, the King reluctantly asked Grenville to form a ministry. Equally reluctantly Grenville accepted, and formed what became known derisively as the 'Ministry of All the Talents', including the best men from all parties. Grenville's ministry lasted just thirteen months and he resigned, as Pitt had done before him, over George III's refusal to accept Catholic emancipation.[11]

Grenville was not a great prime minister for, as he said to his brother, he was 'not competent to the management of men. I never was so naturally, and toil and anxiety more and more unfit me for it'. Yet one of the greatest acts was passed during his ministry—the Abolition of Slavery in 1807.

Although not yet fifty-five, he chose never to hold office again. When he resigned the premiership he wrote to his brother, 'The deed is done and I am again a free man.' He retired to his country estate, Dropmore in Buckinghamshire, speaking only occasionally in the Lords. In 1823 he had a stroke and died in 1834.

Spencer Perceval

Born 1 November 1762
Married Jane Spencer-Wilson
(6 sons, 6 daughters)
Ministry 1809–12 (Tory) – King
George III
Died 11 May 1812. Buried at
Charlton, London

Spencer Perceval was not a great British prime minister, but his name is remembered for the tragic reason that he was shot dead in the House of Commons.

George III was delighted when Perceval succeeded the Duke of Portland as prime minister, for Perceval was a staunch Tory and the King had feared a triumphant return of the Whigs he detested. Despite the King's approval and parliamentary acceptance of his appointment, Perceval's task of forming an administration was not an easy one, since certain ministers refused to serve under him, and his premiership was given only a few months to survive. The country was still at war with France, the Industrial Revolution was gaining strength, the King was ageing and becoming more insane, and the Prince of Wales was made Regent. Perceval battled on for two and half years. Then came the assassin's bullet and Spencer Perceval fell dead in the lobby of the House of Commons on 11 May 1812. The murderer, a merchant named John Bellingham, was arrested immediately, tried on 15 May and hanged outside Newgate Prison on 18 May.

One extraordinary and little-known fact about this murder was that, on the night of 11 May, a Mr Williams, who lived in Redruth, Cornwall, dreamed three times that he was standing in the lobby of the House of Commons and saw a man shoot the prime minister. In the morning he told his friends, who had great difficulty in stopping him from travelling to London to warn the prime minister. A few days later the news reached Cornwall that Perceval had been shot in the lobby. Soon afterwards, Williams was invited to London and shown pictures of the murderer and the scene of the murder. Every detail of the event coincided with the details of his dream.

Perceval was the most reactionary of the nineteenth-century premiers and although a very religious man, upholding the beliefs of the Anglican Church, he still believed in repression of both the Catholics and the working classes. Yet he was honest and uncorrupt, of stainless character in both private and public life and a devoted husband and father.

Lord Liverpool (Robert Banks Jenkinson)

Born 7 June 1770
Married (1) Lady Louisa Hervey
(no children); (2) Mary Chester
(no children)
Ministry 1812–27 (Tory) – King
George III
Died 4 December 1828. Buried
at Hawkesbury, Kent

When the assassin's bullet cut short the life of Spencer Perceval, the King again asked Lord Liverpool to form a ministry. Although reluctant to do so, Liverpool accepted, fearing that his party would suffer if he refused. He remained prime minister for fifteen years—a length of office exceeded only by Walpole and the Younger Pitt before him and never again after him. Yet he is hardly remembered and little is recorded about him.

When he left Oxford in 1789, he had made the grand tour of Europe in common with most young aristocrats of the time, and whilst in Paris he saw the storming of the Bastille[15]—a sight which was to influence his policy towards industrial strife during his ministry. He was a kind, courteous man, well informed and incredibly honest and loyal. Yet his outer calm hid an inner anxiety which George Canning said 'amounted almost to illness'. He was uneasy in company, had few personal friends and was politically a lonely man. He was devoted to his wife, Lady Louisa Hervey, and was deeply distressed when she died in 1821. He was so lonely that the following year he married again.

Lord Liverpool's years of office were not easy ones, but he held on to the leadership, steering the Tories through four general elections and winning them all. During his long premiership, Liverpool also encountered some very turbulent times. The Napoleonic and American wars had to be brought to an end. The King's mental health deteriorated rapidly, until he died in 1820. George IV's immoral behaviour and despicable treatment of his wife Caroline was an embarrassment to Liverpool's administration. Industrial strife was increasing and the first organised strike was staged by Lancashire cotton spinners in

July 1818. In 1819 the Peterloo Massacre[13] took place· which resulted in the Six Acts[14] being passed. In 1820 the Cato Street conspiracy, in which a group of anarchists planned to assassinate the whole Cabinet, was discovered, and the culprits executed. In 1821 Queen Caroline died, and Londoners rioting at her funeral were killed by the military escort. The following year his Foreign Secretary, Robert Castlereagh, committed suicide.

So the colourful administration of a rather uncolourful man continued, until Liverpool suffered a stroke on 17 February 1827. He resigned in April and died on 4 December 1828.

George Canning

Born 11 April 1770
Married Joan Scott (3 sons, 1
daughter)
Ministry 1827 (Tory) – King
George IV
Died 8 August 1827. Buried in
Westminster Abbey

George Canning was prime minister for just one hundred days—a shorter time than any other premier.

He was the son of George and Mary Canning, a couple from Northern Ireland who had come to London after a family quarrel. Canning's early childhood was hard for, after his father's death, his destitute mother went on the stage to support herself and her son, and later married a drunken actor. According to a friend of his mother's, Canning 'was on the road to the gallows'.

Fortunately he was rescued by an uncle, Stratford Canning, a rich City merchant and a staunch Whig, who sent him to Eton and Christ Church, Oxford, where he excelled as a classical scholar and eloquent debater. After Oxford he studied law and was called to the Bar in 1791.

The witty, brilliant Canning was popular among the Whig society to which his uncle had introduced him, and soon he was frequenting the smartest drawing-rooms in London. Then he abandoned his Whig sentiments for the Tory policies of the Younger Pitt, and in July 1793 became MP for Newport, Isle of Wight, and Pitt's most ardent supporter. Canning's star was in the ascendant: in 1796 he became under secretary at the Foreign Office, where he stayed for three years, until he became joint Paymaster General. Pitt then resigned over his Catholic Emancipation Bill[11] defeat, and Canning resigned with him. He refused to serve under Henry Addington, slating his ministry which he called a 'pusillanimous goose administration' and he strove for the reinstatement of Pitt. 'Pitt is to Addington, what London is to Paddington', he jibed. Some years after Pitt's death Canning declared to his constituents: 'To one man while he lived I was devoted with all my heart and soul. Since the death of Mr Pitt I acknowledge no leader.'

Canning was appointed Foreign Secretary in 1807 and he was now able to prove his ability as a statesman. He saved Britain from invasion by boldly sending an expeditionary force to Copenhagen to seize the Danish fleet before it fell into Napoleon's hands. But for all his brilliance, Canning was a cutting critic to all he disliked or despised, and his criticism of Robert Castlereagh, the War Minister, led to a duel on Putney Heath, followed by their respective resignations.

The Duke of Portland resigned the premiership in 1809 and Canning, confident that he would become his successor, was severely disappointed when Spencer Perceval was elected. He refused to serve under the new premier, and almost annihilated his political career when he refused the Foreign Office from Lord Liverpool in 1812. His disappointment was even greater when Castlereagh was appointed as Foreign Secretary and Leader of the House, for Canning himself desired these two offices. In 1814 he became Ambassador to Portugal but within two years realised his foodhardiness and re-entered the Government as President of the Board of Control. He resigned in 1820 over his disapproval of George IV's treatment of Queen Caroline. In 1822 he was prepared to leave for India to take up his appointment as Governor General, when his old enemy Castlereagh committed suicide. Canning replaced him as Foreign Secretary, and the great 'Age of Canning' began.

He disassociated Britain from the Holy Alliance,[16] helped to free Greece from Turkey, and above all helped the Spanish colonies in South America to achieve independence after the

French invasion of Spain. He was determined that France should not conquer Latin America: 'I called the New World into existence to redress the balance of the Old', he claimed.

As Foreign Secretary Canning reigned supreme, although he was not without enemies, for the King disliked him, and the Whigs and the right-wing Tories distrusted him. When Liverpool was forced to resign through ill-health, the ultra-Tories prevailed upon the King to appoint the Duke of Wellington as his successor. On learning of this, Canning approached the King, who, he knew, reserved the right to choose his own ministers, and urged him: 'Sir, your father broke the domination of the Whigs. I hope your Majesty will not endure that of the Tories'. Whereupon the King replied: 'No, I'll be damned if I do.' So, on 10 April 1827, Canning was asked to form a ministry. His task was not easy, however, since Wellington and Robert Peel both refused to serve under him, and he had to depend upon Whig support. Nevertheless, he succeeded in forming his administration, although he had little time to prove his abilities as a prime minister for he died of pneumonia on 8 August 1827.

Whether or not Canning would have proved to be a great prime minister is open to speculation, but he was reputedly a very clever statesman, a brilliant orator, wit and humorist. He supported Catholic Emancipation, but opposed parliamentary reform. He was honest in character and his private life was untainted. He was idyllically happy with his wife, Joan Scott, an heiress who brought him a dowry of £100,000 on their marriage in 1800. He was an excellent father and devoted to his mother, to whom he wrote weekly letters and paid frequent visits.

Lord Goderich (Frederick Robinson)

Born 30 October 1782
Married Lady Sarah Hobart
(2 sons, 1 daughter)
Ministry 1827–8 (Tory) – King
George IV
Died 28 January 1859. Buried
at Nocton, Lincolnshire

Lord Goderich's premiership was an utter failure. He presided for just four months and was described by Disraeli as 'a transient and embarrassed phantom'. But it was not entirely Goderich's fault.

When George Canning died in 1828, his obvious successor was the Duke of Wellington, a staunch ultra-Tory, but the King, wielding the royal prerogative of choosing his own ministers, wanted somebody more politically flexible. He chose Goderich because with his administrative experience and his popularity as a politician, he considered him to be the most likely person to hold the fracturing Tory Party together. But this was not to be. The country's domestic and foreign troubles, the Party's own dissension, and the King's price for his patronage, were all beyond his capabilities. Moreover, Goderich was weak and would burst into tears when things went wrong. Finally the King withdrew his support and Goderich's ministry collapsed in December 1827, leading to his resignation a month later.

Although a nonentity as a prime minister, Goderich was an amenable man and a capable politician who had moved quickly up the political ladder.His contributions to free trade and the country's growing prosperity when he was Chancellor of the Exchequer in Lord Liverpool's administration led William Cobbett, the author of *Rural Rides*, to give him his nickname of Prosperity Robinson.

After his resignation he continued in office for many years and his open-mindedness, optimism and ability to see all sides of a question enabled him to serve in various types of administration.

Duke of Wellington (Arthur Wellesley)

Born 1 May 1769
Married Catherine Pakenham
(2 sons)
Ministry 1828–30 (Tory) – King
George IV
Died 14 September 1852. Buried
in St Paul's Cathedral

When the Duke of Wellington became prime minister after the collapse of Lord Goderich's administration in 1828, he was a national hero, still glorying in his victory over Napoleon at the battle of Waterloo. Although a great soldier, he was not a great politician and he soon became very unpopular and suffered at the hands of rioting mobs, clamouring for fairer parliamentary representation.

Born Arthur Wellesley, he was the fourth son and sixth child of the 1st Earl and Countess of Mornington. His father, who had been a Professor of Music at Trinity College, Dublin, died when Arthur was twelve, and the shy, lonely boy became increasingly reserved. His mother had little time for him, referring to him as 'that ugly boy Arthur', and preferred instead her eldest son.

Arthur was sent to Eton, but he proved a poor scholar and his mother considered the fees a waste of money. She then sent him to a private tutor in Brussels and later to a military school at Angers, France, as she decided her ugly, clumsy son was only 'fit food for powder' and must enter the Army. Arthur, however, had no desire to be a soldier for he had inherited his father's love of music and was an accomplished violinist. Nevertheless, he carried out his mother's wish, and when he returned from Angers in 1787, his brother secured him a commission as an ensign in a Highland regiment. Through his brother's influence promotion came quickly and, in 1793, the family sold part of their estate to buy him a commission as lieutenant-colonel in the 33rd Foot. By now Arthur was content to make soldiering his life and so began the glorious career which was to make him, in the words of Queen Victoria, 'the greatest man this country ever produced, and the most devoted and loyal subject and the staunchest supporter the Crown ever had'.

He fought his first battle in the Flanders' campaign of 1794 after which he was to remark 'I learned what one ought not to do, and that is always something'. In 1796 he went to India, where his brother was Governor General, and directed the wars against the Mahrattas,[17] successfully bringing peace to India and establishing British rule by December 1804. He was knighted for his achievements and returned to England the following year a very rich man.

Wellington became MP for Rye in 1806 and a year later the Duke of Portland appointed him Chief Secretary of Ireland.

Then followed his victorious campaigns in the Peninsular and Napoleonic Wars, culminating in the Battle of Waterloo in 1815. Meantime, he had been made a viscount, fiield marshal, then a duke and Ambassador to Paris. The country had bestowed upon him every military and civil accolade, and rewarded him with grants totalling £500,000. In 1817 the nation presented him with Stratfield Saye, an enormous estate in Hampshire, and he himself purchased Apsley House at Hyde Park Corner, London, now the Wellington Museum.

After the battle of Waterloo, Wellington became Commander-in-Chief of the allied army of occupation in France. He returned to England in 1818 and became Master-general of Ordnance in Lord Liverpool's administration until the resignation of Lord Goderich in 1828, when the King asked him to form a government. Although reluctant, he considered it his duty, and became prime minister on 8 January 1828.

During the second year of his ministry, 1829, he passed the Catholic Relief Bill.[11] He told the House of Lords that he had changed his mind about Catholic emancipation as he saw no alternative to it but civil war: 'if I could avoid, by any sacrifice whatever, even one month of civil war I would sacrifice my life to do it'. Lord Winchilsea accused him of double-dealing and this charge led to Wellington challenging Winchilsea to a duel, which was fought in Battersea Park.

If the Duke had changed his mind about Catholic emancipation, however, he would not change his mind about parliamentary reform. He believed firmly in the ruling classes and that extending the vote to the majority would pave the way to anarchy and mob rule. Opposition grew stronger, but the Duke stood firm: '. . . as long as I hold any station in the government of the country, I shall always feel it my duty to resist such measures'. The popularity of the great hero waned overnight; he was jeered at by mobs who also stoned the windows of his house. Shortly, the Government was defeated in the House of Commons; Wellington resigned and was succeeded by the Whig Earl Grey.

For the next few years the Duke was in opposition, fighting against parliamentary reform, but he finally advised his followers in the Lords to agree to the bill, which was passed on 7 June 1832. A week later, on the seventeenth anniversary of the battle of Waterloo, the Duke was jeered at as he rode to his house. 'An odd day to choose', he commented.

Nevertheless, Wellington recaptured the hero's spirit and was installed as Chancellor of Oxford University and made Warden of the Cinque Ports. William IV invited him to become prime minister again following the dismissal of Melbourne in 1834, but the Duke declined in favour of Robert Peel, and became Foreign Secretary. In Peel's second ministry of 1841 he became Leader of the House of Lords and retired from active politics with Peel's resignation in 1846.

Wellington died whilst sitting in an armchair at Walmer Castle, the residence of the Warden of the Cinque Ports, on 14 September 1852.

As a soldier the Duke was unequalled, but this success was not matched in his private life. He had few men friends and could be unjust to his subordinates. His marriage to Catherine Pakenham was unsuccessful and he reputedly had many affairs. He loved the company of women and was very affectionate towards children. He was a great disciplinarian who showed no emotion whatsoever; generous, never refusing the many charities that prevailed upon him; honest and religious, believing that the Lord's Prayer 'contained the sum total of religion and of morals', this being the creed he lived by.

Earl Grey (Charles Grey)

Born 13 March 1764
Married Elizabeth Ponsonby
(10 sons, 5 daughters)
Ministry 1830–4 (Whig) – King
William IV
Died 17 July 1845. Buried at
Howick, Northumberland

Earl Grey was not one of the greatest prime ministers, but he was responsible for one of the greatest acts, Parliamentary Reform,[18] which opened the way for today's parliamentary system. In direct contrast to the Duke of Wellington, whom he succeeded, and who was opposed to parliamentary reform, he believed 'the rights of man as the foundation of every government, and those who stand against those rights as conspirators against the people'.

When he became prime minister, Grey brought the Whigs out of opposition for the first time for twenty-three years. Within four days he formed a strong ministry containing past and future prime ministers—Goderich, Melbourne, Palmerston, Stanley and Russell. Then began the long and difficult fight for parliamentary reform, culminating in his resignation on 9 May 1832 when the Lords rejected his third Reform Bill. The Duke of Wellington could not form a government and Grey was reinstated, with permission from the King to create new peers if necessary to push the bill through. This power was not required as Wellington, then leader of the Lords, finally advised his followers to vote for it. So Grey's dream was realised and the Parliamentary Reform Act was passed on 7 June 1832.

Grey then set about effecting other reforms. He passed the first Factory Act in 1833, which prevented children under the age of nine from working in factories and restricted the working hours of those under the age of thirteen to forty-eight per week. The Poor Law Amendment Act also was passed and slavery was abolished in the British colonies. He felt his job was now completed, and resigned on 9 July 1834 over the introduction of a new Coercion Bill for Ireland.

He was a diffident, timorous man who wanted peace at any price. A fine, classical scholar from Eton and Cambridge and an honourable, proud, old-fashioned type Whig, who cared for the masses of ordinary people. His home life was ecstatically happy and he hated leaving his family for the four-day journey from Howick to Parliament. Parting from them made him ill and his wife had to persuade him to go. When his life's ambition was achieved, he retired from politics to spend the rest of his days with them at Howick. He died on 17 July 1845.

Lord Melbourne (William Lamb)

Born 15 March 1779
Married Lady Caroline
Ponsonby (1 son)
Ministry 1834; 1835–41 (Whig)
– King William IV, Queen
Victoria
Died 24 November 1848. Buried
at Hatfield, Hertfordshire

But for the advent of Queen Victoria's reign, Lord Melbourne might well have slipped into obscurity. He was the new Queen's first prime minister and to him fell the task of teaching her the intricacies of politics and training her for the long reign ahead of her. She was devoted to him from the beginning, confiding to her diary: 'I like him very much and feel confidence in him.'

They developed an intimate friendship with Victoria becoming possessive and demanding, resenting his relationships with older women. She expected him to visit her every day and depended upon his advice in both her private and official life. He sustained her through the ordeal of her coronation, advised her on the choice of a husband and saw her through the scandals and difficulties of her early years. With the Queen, Melbourne could not fail. And Melbourne, too, was glad to share his inherent solicitousness and affection after the failure of his marriage to Lady Caroline, who had an affair with the poet Byron and became mentally unstable after watching his funeral pass by.

Born William Lamb, he was the second son of Peniston Lamb, 1st Viscount Melbourne and his wife Elizabeth, although it was rumoured that he was the son of Lady Melbourne's regular lover, Lord Egremont. But be that as it may, he became heir to the title on the death of his elder brother in 1805. Educated at Eton and Trinity College, Cambridge, he studied law at Lincoln's Inn and was called to the Bar in 1804. The following year, on the death of his brother, he inherited the family title and abandoned law, in which he had little interest, for a political career. In 1806 he took his seat as member for Leominster.

Melbourne did not hold office until 1827, when he became

Chief Secretary for Ireland in Canning's ministry. His carefree, witty personality, coupled with his support of Catholic emancipation,[11] made him a great favourite in Dublin, and he held this post until he resigned in 1828 when the ultra-Tory Wellington became prime minister. In 1829 his father died and he was elevated to the House of Lords as Viscount Melbourne and a year later became Home Secretary in Lord Grey's administration.

At this time the country was troubled by the progress of the Industrial Revolution, the workers were plotting and demonstrating against the machinery that was destroying their jobs. Melbourne was unsympathetic towards the working classes and, after a riot in which farm labourers had burned hayricks and destroyed their agricultural machinery, he gave his authority to the magistrates to deal with the hundreds of rioters who had been arrested. As a result nearly one thousand people were imprisoned or transported, and nine were hanged. The transportation of the Tolpuddle Martyrs[20] also occurred whilst Melbourne was Home Secretary.

Although he was unpopular in the country, Melbourne was considered by his colleagues to be the only suitable politician to take over the premiership after Earl Grey's resignation in 1834. He was reluctant to accept William IV's request to form a ministry, considering the position 'a damned bore', but Thomas Young, his private secretary, advised him that if his ministry lasted only a couple of months it would have been worth being prime minister of England. 'Such a position', he commented, 'was never occupied by any Greek or Roman.'

'By God, you're right', said Melbourne. 'I'll do it.' So, on 16 July 1834, Melbourne became prime minister. His ministry was shortlived, for the King dismissed him the following November in favour of Robert Peel, but when Peel's ministry collapsed five months later, the King reluctantly recalled Melbourne. Equally reluctantly Melbourne accepted, and in April 1835 he formed his second administration. His government was weak, and Melbourne himself was not very popular. His love affairs were causing scandal and he was cited as co-respondent by George Norton, a Tory MP, in his divorce case. Despite the fact that the judge ruled in favour of Melbourne, the damage was done to his already floundering ministry, and it was generally believed that it could not survive for long. However, a few months later, King William died, Victoria became Queen, and Melbourne's

52

successful life as her first minister began. He was installed at Windsor Castle where he remained until his resignation in 1841 after a series of government defeats.

Melbourne's retirement from politics and his royal duties was an emotional occasion for himself and the Queen, even though she now had her consort to sustain her; nevertheless he refused her offer of the Garter. Victoria kept in touch with Melbourne by correspondence and invited him to Windsor during his retirement at Brocket Hall, his country home in Hertfordshire. A highly intelligent, well read man he never held office again, and spent his time among his books. He died on 24 November 1848.

Sir Robert Peel

Born 5 February 1788
Married Julia Floyd (5 sons, 2 daughters)
Ministry 1834–5; 1841–6 (Tory)
– King William IV, Queen Victoria
Died 2 July 1850. Buried at Drayton Bassett

Queen Victoria called him that cold, odd man, who was not quite a gentleman; the Irish Catholics named him Orange Peel; his wife said he 'was the light of my life, my brightest joy and pride', and Disraeli said he was 'the greatest member of Parliament that ever lived'. The man who collected these titles was Robert Peel, the first prime minister to come from the Industrial Revolution's *nouveau riche*.

There was never any doubt as to what career he should follow. His father, a rich cotton miller and Tory MP for Tamworth, had trained him from an early age to be a politician. As a small boy he was often asked to make a speech, and every Sunday he was required to repeat the sermon on returning from church. This was the origin of his ability to recall *verbatim* his opponents' arguments in debate.

Peel was educated at Harrow and Christ Church, Oxford, where he became the first person to gain a double first—in classics and mathematics. In 1809, he entered the House of Commons as member for Cashel, Tipperary. Within a year, Spencer Perceval made him Under Secretary for War and, two years later, Lord Liverpool appointed him Chief Secretary for Ireland—one of the toughest jobs in the government. Ireland was full of poverty, which bred discontent and conspiracy and Peel, opposed to Catholic emancipation,[11] was not popular. The Catholics named him Orange Peel, believing him to be a Protestant Orangeman and Daniel O'Connell, their leader, said his smile 'was like the silver plate on a coffin'. But Peel stayed in Dublin for six years.

In 1818 he resigned and remained out of office until he became Home Secretary in 1822. During his five years at the Home Office, he reduced the number of capital crimes from nearly two hundred to eight. He resigned in 1827, as he would not serve under George Canning, but in 1828 became Home Secretary again and Leader of the House of Commons, under Wellington. He was converted to Catholic emancipation[11] and was instrumental in pushing the Catholic Emancipation Bill through Parliament. This cost him his seat at Oxford University, which he had represented for eleven years. He then represented Westbury, exchanging this seat for Tamworth in 1830.

In 1829 Peel established himself firmly in history by creating the Metropolitan Police Force (hence the nickname Bobby or Peeler for the British policeman). With the fall of Wellington's Government in 1830 Peel was relegated to the opposition and at the same time his father died and he succeeded to his baronetcy. In opposition Peel was against parliamentary reform, although he believed that some change should be carried out, but slowly. When Earl Grey resigned in July 1834 the King asked Peel to form a coalition with Melbourne, but Peel declined and went to Italy. When Melbourne was dismissed the following November the King sent a message to Italy to again ask Peel to become prime minister. This time he accepted. He dissolved Parliament at once, hoping for a large Tory majority. At the general election that followed he made his famous speech to his constituents at Tamworth, in which he stated that the Reform Act must be accepted but that the Government would be conservative and retain what was good of the old ways. This speech became known as the Tamworth Manifesto, and so was born the Conservative Party as opposed to the old Tories. Peel did not gain the huge majority he had hoped for, however, and his Government was repeatedly defeated; he resigned in April 1835.

Melbourne again became prime minister but Peel led the opposition. He was a much respected member and the House always fell silent when he rose to speak. When Melbourne resigned in June 1841 Peel became premier despite the fact that the Queen disliked him. (Melbourne had taught Victoria that as a constitutional monarch it was her duty to accept as her prime minister the man chosen by the majority of the Commons— William IV, her predecessor, having been the last monarch to choose his own ministers.)

When Peel took office the country was in a bad state—trade was poor, unemployment was high, the working classes were depressed and foreign affairs were troublesome. He formed a strong ministry and set out his tasks. He reduced tariffs on many articles and abolished others; then to offset the loss of Government revenue he introduced an income tax of 7d (3p) in the pound. This free trade policy succeeded and the country prospered. He passed the Mines Act (1842), forbidding the employment of women and children in the mines; the Factory Act (1844), limiting the working hours of women and children; the Railway Act (1844), requiring the railways to provide penny-a-mile daily services, and the Bank Charter Act (1844), regulating the number of bank notes printed and gold stocks held by the Bank of England.

It seemed that Peel, the great reformer, could do no wrong, and even Queen Victoria warmed to him, regarding him as her trusted friend. But then came the rains of 1845 and disaster for Peel. The harvest failed and people were clamouring for the repeal of the corn laws,[19] passed in 1815, forbidding the import of cheap foreign corn, and thus keeping up the price of British corn. Peel knew that these laws must go, but he could not oppose the majority of his party who did not agree with him.

His humanity prevailed when the Irish potato crop—on which the Irish depended for their food, not being able to afford bread —was struck by blight and nearly a million people died in the resulting famine and another million fled to America. Peel sent food to Ireland, but it was not enough to prevent starvation. He decided then, albeit reluctantly, that wheat would have to be

55

imported and the corn laws would have to be repealed. When he announced his proposals to the House there was uproar. His party, apart from Lord Aberdeen and Gladstone, refused to support him. Peel, believing he could not carry on, resigned. Both Lord John Russell and Lord Stanley failed in their attempts to form ministries, and Peel resumed his premiership with all his ministers, except Lord Stanley, agreeing to serve with him.

The ensuing debate, which was extremely hostile, lasted for five months. Peel was accused of betraying his party, Melbourne told the Queen it 'was a damned dishonest act' and Disraeli, whom Peel had omitted from his Cabinet, took his revenge, hurling abuse at him and denouncing Peel as a traitor. Unbearable though it was, Peel did not relent, and, on 25 June 1846, the corn laws were repealed. His triumph was shortlived for, on the night of that historic day, Peel was defeated over an Irish Coercion Bill. He resigned and never held office again.

Peel spent most of his retirement at his house in Drayton Bassett with his wife and their seven children. His marriage was extremely happy and his wife, who had confessed that she 'was no politician', became his closest friend and the only person with whom he shared his inmost thoughts. Soon after his marriage Peel became a collector of great paintings, owning almost 150 masterpieces, most of which are in the National Gallery, London.

Peel's last speech in the House of Commons was on 28 June 1850 when he attacked Lord Palmerston's foreign policy on Greece. The next day, whilst riding along Constitution Hill, he was thrown from his horse. He was taken to his home in Whitehall Gardens, where he died in great pain on 2 July.

Lord John Russell (Earl Russell)

Born 18 August 1792
Married (1) Adelaide Lister,
Lady Ribblesdale (2 daughters);
(2) Lady Fanny Elliot (3 sons,
1 daughter)
Ministry 1846–51; 1865–6
(Whig) – Queen Victoria
Died 28 May 1878. Buried at
Chenies, Buckinghamshire

Lord John Russell was known as Little Johnny, for he stood not much higher than Queen Victoria. He was a firm believer in civil and religious liberty and spent his life championing every cause that would benefit the people.

The third son of the 6th Duke of Bedford, he was educated at Westminster School and Edinburgh University—the first prime minister to come from a university other than Oxford or Cambridge. In 1813 he became MP for Tavistock, but ill-health and despondency over his chances of success because of the Tory majority, soon prompted him to think of giving up politics for literature; but his friends persuaded him to persevere.

Setting his sights on parliamentary reform, he helped to draft the Reform Bill[18] which passed through Parliament in 1832. In Lord Melbourne's second administration he became first, Leader of the House of Commons and Home Secretary, and later Colonial Secretary. When Peel took office in 1841, Russell led the opposition and supported the repeal of the corn laws.[19] Peel resigned over this issue in December 1845 but Russell was unable to form a ministry, so Peel resumed his premiership. But when Peel was defeated the following June the Queen again asked Russell to form a ministry and this time he succeeded.

Unlike Peel's, his administration was not a strong one. Palmerston was his Foreign Secretary, and the Queen did not like Palmerston. She suggested that Russell should restrain his power as he was becoming a law unto himself. Russell, however, was preoccupied with his own affairs, for the country was in an unhappy state—trade was poor, unemployment was high and Ireland was ravaged by famine. He immediately introduced coercive measures to help Ireland, set about adapting a free-trade policy to avoid a workers' revolution, and passed the Factory Act (1847) limiting the daily working hours of women to ten. In December 1851 he asked Palmerston to resign for recognising Louis Napoleon's coup d'état. Two months later, Palmerston had his 'tit for tat with Johnny Russell' as he called it, by defeating him on the Militia Bill and causing his resignation (see p 64).

The Earl of Derby then became prime minister for ten months, and Russell was in opposition. In December 1852, Lord Aberdeen formed his coalition ministry, and Russell became Foreign Secretary and Leader of the House of Commons. He was not very successful and was blamed for a lot of the failure during the Crimean War, a war of which he fiercely disapproved. He resigned in January 1855, lost popularity and was out of office until June 1859 when he became Foreign Secretary again in Palmerston's ministry, and championed the cause for a united Italy.

In 1861 he was elevated to the House of Lords as Earl Russell of Kingston Russell, and the following year given the Garter. When Palmerston died in October 1865, the Queen again asked him to take office: 'The Queen can turn to none other than Lord Russell, an old and tried friend, to undertake the arduous duties of Prime Minister and carry on the Government', she wrote to him. Although seventy-three years of age, Russell felt it his duty to accept and he formed his administration with Gladstone as his Chancellor of the Exchequer. The following year he introduced a new Reform Bill, which was defeated, and he gladly took the opportunity to resign. He never held office again, although it was repeatedly offered to him. He died on 28 May 1878.

Russell, who was the grandfather of the philosopher Bertrand Russell, was a widely travelled, cultured, literary man. A splendid husband and devoted father to his many children and step-children, he did not marry until he was forty-three. His wife, Adelaide Lister, the widow of Lord Ribblesdale, who had four children by her first marriage, died soon after their second child was born. He married his second wife when she was twenty-five and he was forty-nine. Their marriage was very happy and they lived at Pembroke Lodge in Richmond Park, a grace-and-favour residence granted them by Queen Victoria.

Earl of Derby (Edward George Stanley)

Born 29 March 1799
Married Emma Bootle-
Wilbraham (2 sons, 1 daughter)
Ministry 1852; 1858–9; 1866–8
(Conservative) – Queen Victoria
Died 23 October 1869. Buried
at Knowsley

The Earl of Derby was the first man to hold office three separate times as prime minister, yet he remains a shadowy figure in the annals of British premierships. He was reluctant to accept the responsibilities of office, preferring instead the pursuits of leisure. He was a great gambler and trained the famous Derby race-horses. But he never managed to achieve his ambition to win the Derby or the St Leger.

The eldest son of the 13th Earl of Derby, he was born into a staunchly Whig, old aristocratic family. He was educated at Eton and Christ Church, Oxford, where he excelled as a Latin and classical scholar. As eldest sons of peers were expected to do in those days, he dutifully entered Parliament when he came of age in 1820. He served in the governments of George Canning, Lord Goderich and Earl Grey, but, in 1835, he abandoned the Whigs and became a Conservative under Robert Peel. He declined invitations to join Peel's first ministry, but accepted the post of Colonial Secretary in Peel's second ministry in 1841.

In 1844 Derby was elevated to the House of Lords as Baron Stanley. He resigned as Colonial Secretary in 1846 when Peel proposed immediate free trade, and became the Leader of the Protectionists[21] in the House of Lords. For the next six years he was in opposition during Lord Russell's Whig ministry. By now he had succeeded his father as Earl Derby (1851) and had made several brilliant speeches on foreign affairs.

When Lord Palmerston defeated Lord John Russell over the Militia Bill in February 1852 (see p 64), the Queen asked Derby to become prime minister. He formed a very weak ministry which lasted ten months, being defeated over the budget of his Chancellor, Disraeli, the following December.

During his second ministry he abolished the property qualifica-tions for MPs, settled the murder conspiracy dispute with France,[22] removed Jewish disabilities, and transferred the govern-ment of India from the East India Company[12] to the Crown. Derby's government was defeated a second time as a result of Disraeli's efforts as Chancellor, this time introducing a bill to extend the voting rights of professional men.

For the next seven years, Derby was in opposition. Then in July 1866, when Russell had been defeated over Gladstone's Reform Bill, he became Prime Minister for the third time. Again Disraeli was his Chancellor of the Exchequer and between them they pushed through parliament the second Reform Bill which received the Royal Assent on 9 August 1867. Just over six months later, on 25 February 1868, Derby resigned through ill-health. He died on 23 October 1869.

During almost fifty years in parliament he had been a Whig, Canningite, Whig leader, Peelite, Protectionist and Conservative leader. This inconsistency had earned him a reputation as a turncoat, but he was consistent in his views on Catholic emancipation[11] and parliamentary reform, which he always favoured. He was a great fighter and would enter the foray for the fight itself rather than the cause he was fighting for. He was highly intellectual and very offhand and aloof to anyone not his social equal. His literary achievements included various translations of ancient and modern poems and also a translation in blank verse of Homer's *Iliad*. During the Lancashire cotton famine of 1862–4 he was chairman of the relief committee which was established, and helped to raise the necessary monetary target to which he contributed generously himself.

Earl of Aberdeen (George Hamilton Gordon)

Born 28 January 1784
Married (1) Lady Catherine
Hamilton (3 daughters); (2)
Viscountess Harriet Hamilton
(2 sons)
Ministry 1852–5 (Tory) – Queen
Victoria
Died 14 December 1860. Buried
at Stanmore, Middlesex

When the Earl of Aberdeen accepted Queen Victoria's invitation to head a coalition ministry after the collapse of Lord Derby's administration in December 1852, she wrote and told her uncle, King Leopold of the Belgians, how happy she was to have 'my faithful friend Aberdeen' as prime minister. But the faithful friend was not successful as a prime minister and, like Lord North nearly a century before him, was to take much of the blame for a war which he considered to be 'most unwise and unnecessary'.

60

Aberdeen was educated at Harrow and St John's College, Cambridge, where he excelled as a classical scholar in both arts and antiquities. Later he became a trustee of the National Gallery and British Museum, and President of the Society of Antiquaries. After graduating, he made the grand tour of Europe, extending his travels to Greece and carrying out archaeological digs in Athens and Ephesus. He succeeded as 4th Earl of Aberdeen in 1801 and four years later, when he was twenty-one, he came into his inheritance.

Aberdeen became British Ambassador in Vienna in 1813 and was instrumental in persuading Austria's Emperor, Francis I, to join the Allies against France. He witnessed some of the bitterest battles of the final stages of the Napoleonic Wars and developed an abhorrence for the carnage of war as a result. In May 1815 he signed the Treaty of Paris for Britain which ended the Napoleonic Wars, and a month later was rewarded for his services with a peerage.

He devoted the next fourteen years to his private life, returning to Parliament in 1828 after which he held various posts until he became Foreign Secretary in Peel's second ministry of 1841. Succeeding the pugnacious Palmerston, he set out on a pacific policy, creating friendly relations with France and settling an old boundary dispute with the United States. He supported parliamentary reform, Catholic emancipation[11] and Peel's abolition of the corn laws.[19] He resigned with Peel in 1841, and on Peel's death in 1850, he became leader of the Peelites and, two years later, prime minister of a coalition government.

Aberdeen's cabinet was a strong one which included Gladstone from the Peelite Tories and Lords Palmerston and Russell from the Whigs. But this talent was too strong for Aberdeen's ineffectual leadership and, through mismanagement of the Middle East crisis, the country drifted into the Crimean War in March 1854—a war which claimed the lives of hundreds of British soldiers and brought down Aberdeen's coalition government on 30 January 1855. After his resignation in 1855, he never held office again.

Although Aberdeen was a failure as prime minister, his political and personal life was far from unsuccessful. He was a beneficent landlord, spending much time and money on the welfare and happiness of his tenants. He was a devoted father and husband, and both his marriages were supremely happy. He described his first wife as the most perfect creature that God had ever made, and was griefstricken when she died in 1812 seven years after their marriage. Three years later, he married the widow of his first wife's brother. He died on 14 December 1860 and is buried at Stanmore.

Viscount Palmerston (Henry John Temple)

Born 20 October 1784
Married Lady Emily Cowper
(no children)
Ministry 1855–8; 1859–65
(Liberal) – Queen Victoria
Died 18 October 1865. Buried
in Westminster Abbey

Lord Palmerston was possibly the most colourful character in Parliament since Walpole. Loved by the people, hated by the Queen, disapproved of by Peel and Gladstone, he was a law unto himself.

The eldest son of the 2nd Viscount Palmerston, he was educated at Harrow and Cambridge. He succeeded his father in 1802 and, as the title was an Irish one—first bestowed upon his grandfather by Sir Robert Walpole in 1722—it did not prevent him from sitting in the House of Commons. In 1807, through family influence, he became Junior Lord of the Admiralty, giving him a seat in the Government before he even entered Parliament. A few months later, he was elected Tory MP for Newport, Isle of Wight. In 1809, Spencer Perceval offered him the Chancellorship of the Exchequer, but he declined this in favour of the War Office, believing he could exercise his excellent business acumen as Secretary for War and still find time for his social and sporting activities. He was very popular among society, especially with the ladies who nicknamed him 'Cupid'.

Palmerston was not particularly ambitious and like most young aristocrats of his day, he fulfilled his political obligations as a duty to his country. But he was well suited to his post in the

War Office, since he stayed there, despite invitations to accept other offices, for nineteen years—serving under five prime ministers—until 1828, when the Canningites resigned from the Duke of Wellington's Government, and Palmerston resigned with them.

A supporter of Catholic emancipation[11] and parliamentary reform, Palmerston left the Tories and joined the Whigs. For the next two years he was out of office, but was appointed Foreign Secretary by Earl Grey, who became prime minister in November 1830. This was an ideal post for Palmerston who was interested in foreign affairs, had travelled much in Europe, and could speak French, Italian and German. He soon established his position. British to his fingertips and extremely chauvinistic, he was not afraid to tell other nations what he thought of them. His aggressive policy brought the disapproval of Peel and Gladstone who regarded him as a bully. Palmerston believed it was his duty to protect the interests of Britain, to keep her at peace in order to preserve her free trading position, and that the best way of preserving peace was to keep an equal balance of power. Any nation which displeased him was threatened with the British fleet— knowing that the British Navy was the most powerful in the world, he used it as a deterrent. He did not respect other nations or their sovereigns and would despatch offensive letters or his warships without consulting anybody. This offended the Queen who had family interests in most parts of Europe.

Palmerston's main concern was to keep France and Russia in check. His first job as Foreign Secretary was to effect the independence of Belgium and to instal Queen Victoria's uncle, Leopold, as the first king in 1830. Three years later he made an alliance with France and ended the civil wars in Spain and Portugal. He saved Turkey from Russia, who had declared war on her during the Greek War of Independence. Through his *Opium War* with China, when he sent ships to bombard Canton after the Chinese had confiscated English merchants' smuggled opium, he effected a trade agreement with China through which he procured Hong Kong for the British. Britain was at the height of her power—one of the richest nations, she ruled a mighty empire and her people were proud of her, and of the man who protected her.

Palmerston's powerful position was shaken, however, over an incident that occurred in Athens in 1849 when a mob destroyed the home of Don Pacifico, a Gibraltar-born Jewish money-lender. The Greeks refused him compensation and, being a British subject, he appealed to Palmerston for help. Palmerston rose to Don Pacifico's defence, sent in the fleet and threatened to attack if the Greeks did not offer compensation. There was an outcry in the Commons and it seemed certain that Palmerston would be forced to resign. However, he defended his policy in a five-hour speech, during which he maintained that any British subject, whoever he might be, was entitled to British protection. This brought cheers of approbation from the House and Palmerston emerged triumphant.

Palmerston overreached himself in December 1851, however, when he acknowledged Louis Napoleon as Emperor of France. The Queen demanded of the prime minister, Lord John Russell, that he be dismissed. Russell had no choice, and Palmerston was removed from the Foreign Office. Two months later, in February 1852, Palmerston proposed an amendment to the Militia Bill, which forced the resignation of Lord Russell, and achieved what he called 'my tit-for-tat with Johnny Russell'.

Palmerston stayed out of office during Derby's ministry, having declined the Chancellorship of the Exchequer, but he later became Home Secretary in Lord Aberdeen's coalition—the Queen had no objection to him being there, if he had to be anywhere. He maintained an interest in foreign affairs and advised Aberdeen to take a strong line with Russia over her harassment of Turkey. Had Aberdeen heeded his advice the Crimean War might well have been averted, but Britain was plunged into war, the first to be reported by the press. When the country learned of the horrifying conditions of the soldiers they demanded that Aberdeen should resign and that Palmerston should lead the country. And so 'Old Pam', as he was called, took over the premiership on 4 February 1855, at the age of seventy-one.

His critics predicted a short life for his ministry, but they had forgotten their Palmerston—he knew parliamentary procedure, he knew how to manage the press, and he stayed where he was (with one short break) for eleven years. He ended the Crimean War, and signed the Treaty of Paris in 1856, whereby Russia agreed not to keep ships in the Black Sea, and survived the Indian Mutiny.[23] But in February 1858 he resigned over the defeat of his Conspiracy to Murder Bill.[22]

Palmerston remained in opposition during Derby's second administration, but, when the Liberals (as the Whigs were now known) won the election on 18 June 1859, he again became prime minister and remained in office until he died on 18 October 1865, just two days before his eighty-first birthday.

Swashbuckling, 'Old Pam', self-confident, imperious, this beautifully dressed, witty dandy, held the British Empire, like Atlas, upon his shoulders. Foreign nations dreaded him: 'If the devil has a son, surely it is Palmerston', groaned the Germans. But the British people loved him. He never seemed to grow old and could enjoy the company of young and old alike, and his wife, Lady Emily Cowper, whom he married when he was fifty-five, was always ready to support him. Typical of his challenging spirit, when he fell ill on 12 October 1865, and his doctor told him he was going to die, he said, 'Die, that's the *last* thing I shall do'.

Benjamin Disraeli (Earl of Beaconsfield)

Born 21 December 1804
Married Mary Anne Lewis (no children)
Ministry 1868; 1874–80 (Conservative) – Queen Victoria
Died 19 April 1881. Buried at Hughenden, Buckinghamshire

When Benjamin Disraeli kissed Queen Victoria's hands as prime minister, he told her 'I plight my troth to the kindest of Mistresses'. Victoria, glad to be rid of those 'two dreadful old men', Palmerston and Russell, was delighted. Not since Melbourne had she had a prime minister with whom she had such rapport, who made her feel good to be a woman. She called him 'Dizzy', he called her 'the faery', an odd name indeed for a plump, middle-aged widow. But, the sycophantic Disraeli remarked to a friend: 'Everyone likes flattery, but when it comes to royalty you must lay it on with a trowel'—and 'lay it on' he did. He had come to the 'top of the greasy pole', as he put it, and he intended to enjoy it.

His climb had been a tough one, for he was not born or bred a gentleman. The eldest son of Isaac D'Israeli, an Italian-Jewish author, he had been baptised into the Church of England at St Andrews, Holborn, on 31 July 1817, when he was twelve years old. He had little formal education, attending three different private schools before he was fifteen. He was articled to a solicitor and later entered Lincoln's Inn, but abandoned law as he wanted to become a famous man—and lawyers rarely became famous men. He was now twenty years old and extremely ambitious. He gambled on the Stock Exchange with South American mining shares and helped his father's friend, John Murray the publisher, to start *The Representative*, a newspaper to rival *The Times*. Both enterprises failed with the result that Disraeli was heavily in debt, and John Murray lost thousands of pounds.

He then wrote his first book, *Vivian Grey*, a brilliantly witty, politico-social novel. Published anonymously in April 1826, it was immediately successful, with the gossips fitting real-life characters to his satirised fictional ones, and John Murray suspected of being the central character. When Disraeli was exposed as the author, the wrath of London's literary circle came down upon him. He then suffered a nervous breakdown and went to live quietly at his father's house in Bradenham in Buckinghamshire, where he continued to write until 1830 when he set out on a tour of Europe. His health improved, and in 1831 he returned determined to become a politician and man-about-town. He set up home in St James's Street off Piccadilly in London, took a mistress, dressed in flamboyant clothes and spoke and behaved in an affected manner. He was determined to be seen and heard. At a party in 1834 he met Lord Melbourne who, liking him on sight, asked him what he wanted to be. 'Prime minister' answered Disraeli, who was not then even a politician.

Five times he stood for Parliament before being elected member for Maidstone in November 1837, when he entered the House of Commons as a follower of Peel. He made his first speech—a complete disaster—on an Irish motion, on 7 December. With his odd clothes and long black ringlets hanging round his thin, dark-complexioned face, he was ridiculed mercilessly by most of the House. Sitting down amid jeers, he said with confidence, 'The time will come when you *will* hear me'. Peel was among the few who did not laugh at him, but it was Peel who eventually suffered from his vicious tongue.

At the general election in 1841 Disraeli was returned as member for Shrewsbury. By now he was regarded as a brilliantly witty, very able Tory, and he was sure he would be included in Peel's cabinet. His rejection made him determined to seek revenge, and this he did in 1846 during the debate on the repeal of the corn laws.[19] For months he vilified Peel, denouncing him as a traitor and a hypocrite. The corn laws were repealed by Peel on 25 June 1846 but, on that very night, Disraeli forced the resignation of Peel's Government by voting, with his followers, against an Irish Coercion Bill. Disraeli then became leader of the shattered Conservative Party.

Two years later, in 1848, he bought Hughenden Manor in Buckinghamshire, and represented this county in Parliament. In February 1852 he won a seat in the Government when Lord Derby appointed him Leader of the House of Commons and Chancellor of the Exchequer. In this post he was responsible for the nightly letter to the Queen informing her of the day's procedure in the House. Victoria loved his style of writing and became interested in him.

The defeat of his budget in December 1852 caused the downfall of Derby's government and put Disraeli out of office until he again became Chancellor under Derby in 1858. This time he introduced a new Reform Bill, which was rejected, and the government resigned. In Derby's administration of 1866 Disraeli became Chancellor for the third time. Russell's Liberal Government had resigned over the defeat of Gladstone's Reform Bill. Disraeli, mainly responsible for its defeat, introduced yet another Bill giving the vote to the industrial working classes. Disraeli had triumphed. Gladstone called him 'diabolically clever', but the Queen and the country highly approved of him. When the ailing Derby resigned in February 1868, Victoria unhesitatingly asked Disraeli to become prime minister. He had achieved his ambition and on 27 February 1868 an ecstatic Disraeli announced, 'I have climbed to the top of the greasy pole'.

His first ministry was shortlived and he was defeated by the Liberals at the general election the following December when

Gladstone became prime minister. There was much rivalry between these two great men who were so totally different. Gladstone was physically fit and strong, Disraeli a weakling who suffered from gout. But Gladstone was sombre, long–winded and dull, while Disraeli was bright and witty. To Gladstone he was evil and scheming, and to Disraeli Gladstone was a sanctimonious prig. The Queen offered Disraeli an earldom, which he declined, asking instead for a peerage for his wife, Mary Anne, to whom he was devoted. This was granted and she became Viscountess Beaconsfield. Mary Anne, whom Disraeli had married in August 1839, was the widow of Wyndham Lewis, a rich industrialist. She was twelve years older than Disraeli and used to tease him that he married her for her money. This does not appear to be so, for their marriage was idyllically happy, and Disraeli was griefstricken when she died in September 1872.

Disraeli became prime minister again on 18 February 1874 at the age of 70. To lighten his workload and ease his gout, the Queen made him the Earl of Beaconsfield and he was elevated to the House of Lords. After his first day there he said, 'I am dead. Dead, but in the Elysian Fields.'

His second ministry, in which he introduced a number of social reforms, was eminently successful. The Trade Union Act (1876) allowed the unions peaceful picketing; the Education Act (1880) made attendance at school compulsory for children between the ages of four and ten; the Artisans Dwelling Act (1875) provided housing for the poor, the Climbing Boys Act (1875) made it the business of the police to enforce the acts of 1840 and 1864 abolishing the employment of young children as chimney-sweeps; the Public Health Act (1875) provided water to houses, and refuse collection, and the Merchant Shipping Act (1876) introduced the Plimsoll line[24] for the loading of merchant ships.

Disraeli also triumphed abroad. He acquired almost half the Suez Canal by buying the shares from the Khedive of Egypt in 1875. The following year, 1 May 1876, he was responsible for the proclamation of Queen Victoria as Empress of India. In 1878 the imminence of war with Russia, which had invaded Turkey, caused Disraeli to send the British fleet to the Dardanelles to resist Russian advancement. It was during this episode that the word 'jingoism' (meaning, originally, a supporter of Disraeli's policy) was coined. A music-hall artiste, Charlie Williams (the pseudonym of an aristocratic gentleman disinherited for going on stage) set the country singing his song: *'We don't want to fight, but by Jingo! if we do, we've got the ships, we've got the men, we've got the money too.'* But Britain did not have to fight. War was averted by Disraeli negotiating his 'peace with honour' at the Congress of Berlin in August 1878.

Two years later, at the general election in April 1880, the Conservatives were badly beaten by the Liberals, and Disraeli resigned in favour of Gladstone. Disraeli retired to Hughenden, where he wrote his final novel, *Endymion*. He died of bronchitis on 19 April 1881 and is buried beside his wife in Hughenden churchyard.

The choice Disraeli had to make between devoting his life to writing or to politics was a difficult one, for writing, as he told the Queen, was a 'weakness, which organically, it seems, I cannot resist'. Had he chosen to write solely, he would perhaps have been one of the leading writers of English literature. His novels are original, witty and acutely perceptive, and much can be learned about him from his writing. *Contarini Fleming*, a psychological romance, and *The Wondrous Tale of Alroy*, an historical novel, both reveal his innate pride in his Jewish ancestry. His non-fiction work reveals his faith in democratic conservatism, his belief in social reform and his inestimable pride in the British Empire and the Crown.

Queen Victoria regarded him as one of the best friends she ever had. He it was who coaxed her from her reclusion after Prince Albert's death. When Disraeli died she wrote: 'His devotion and kindness to me, his wise counsels, his great gentleness combined with firmness, his one thought of the honour and glory of the country, make the death of my dear Lord Beaconsfield a national calamity.' The day of his death, 19 April, was named Primrose Day[25] as that was said to be his favourite flower. On his coffin were two wreaths from the Queen—a simple one of primroses, saying simply 'his favourite flower', and a formal one bearing the words 'A token of true affection, friendship, and respect'.

William Ewart Gladstone

Born 19 December 1809
Married Catherine Glynne (4
sons, 4 daughters)
Ministry 1868–74; 1880–5; 1886;
1892–4 (Liberal) – Queen
Victoria
Died 19 May 1898. Buried in
Westminster Abbey

Although William Gladstone became prime minister four times he never managed to gain the affection of Queen Victoria. She detested him, regarding him as a humbug, a 'half-mad firebrand' hardly fit to lead her empire. After the charming Disraeli, she found it difficult to understand Gladstone's cold, formal manner. 'He addresses me', she complained, 'as though I were a public meeting.' She criticised him constantly, interfered in his affairs and always insisted on his standing in her presence, even when he was an old man—something she never made Disraeli do. Gladstone confided to his friends 'the Queen is enough to kill any man', but he never failed to treat her with the greatest respect.

Gladstone, the fourth son of Sir John Gladstone, was educated at Eton and Christ Church, Oxford, where he gained a double first in classics and mathematics. He entered Lincoln's Inn, but was not called to the Bar. Fervently religious, he wanted to take Holy Orders as his one desire was to serve God and mankind. His father persuaded him he could do this equally well in politics and, after a settling of conscience, he was returned as MP for Newark in December 1832. He entered Parliament as an ultra-Tory soon after the great Reform Act,[18] speaking out against most of the reforms, particularly those which allowed dissention from the Church of England. With the publication of his first book, *The State in its Relations with the Church*, in 1838, the historian Macaulay called him 'the rising hope of the

70

stern, unbending Tories'. But during the course of his long career in Parliament, Gladstone, the most Christian of statesmen, was to become the most liberal of Liberals—the 'Grand Old Man' of politics.

He made his first speech during the debate on the abolition of slavery in 1833. Since his father owned slaves on his sugar plantation in Demerera, Gladstone opposed the emancipation of slaves, genuinely believing that it would not be in the interest of the slaves, or the colonies, to free them. His ability as an orator attracted the attention of Peel and, in Peel's first ministry of 1834, Gladstone became a Junior Lord of the Treasury and later Under-Secretary at the Colonial Office. He resigned with Peel, a few months later, and remained in opposition for the next six years.

In Peel's second administration of 1841 Gladstone became Vice-President of the Board of Trade, and then President in 1843. In 1845, when Peel proposed a grant to the Roman Catholic Seminary at Maynooth, Ireland, Gladstone resigned for, although he approved of Peel's plan, he felt he could not support it from within the Government. Peel admitted that he found it very difficult at times to understand Gladstone. Later in the year, Gladstone rejoined Peel's ministry as Colonial Secretary although by now he had lost his seat at Newark and had been out of Parliament during the corn laws debate.[19] With the shattering of the Tory Party in 1846, Gladstone followed Peel, becoming a Liberal Conservative. He now believed in free trade and lost many of his egalitarian principles. In 1847 he was returned to Parliament as member for Oxford University, holding his seat until 1865.

In 1852 he replied to Disraeli's budget speech—a speech which was to establish Gladstone as one of the great orators and which was to be the first of the many verbal duels, extending over a quarter of a century, between those two great men. Gladstone was verbose, long-winded and dull, but always moral, while Disraeli was witty, cutting and vitriolic. With the collapse of the Derby administration in 1853, Gladstone then succeeded Disraeli as Chancellor of the Exchequer in Lord Aberdeen's coalition ministry, and thus began his magnificent career as one of Britain's finest chancellors.

As a financier Gladstone was brilliant, equalling Walpole, Pitt and Peel before him. His first budget, rising from the wreck of

Disraeli's efforts, was a huge success. Following on the work started by Peel, he abolished many tariffs and lowered others. He reduced income tax, pledging to abolish it altogether but, with the outbreak of the Crimean War, of which he disapproved, he was later forced to increase it, and add duty to sugar, malt and spirits to pay for the war. Gladstone was Chancellor again in Palmerston's ministry for six years from 1859, and under Russell from 1865 to 1866.

By now he was completely converted to the Liberal Party, becoming its leader in 1867. When the Liberals won the election in December 1868 the Queen was forced with great reluctance, to ask Gladstone to form a ministry. 'Very significant. My mission is to pacify Ireland,' said Gladstone, wanting to settle the long embittered struggle of that country by granting the Irish home rule. His first step towards this aim was the disestablishment of the Irish Church in 1869, and, the following year, he passed the Land Act in an effort to protect Irish peasants from wealthy landlords.

At home, Gladstone passed the Education Act (1870), establishing school boards to supply elementary education where no parochial schools existed. He introduced educational examinations for entrance to the Civil Service (1870), and passed the Universities Test Act (1871), which made it possible for non-Church of England members to teach at the universities and the Ballot Act (1872), making voting secret. He also abolished the purchasing of commissions in the army. His Trade Union Act (1871) gave the unions legal status and his Licensing Act (1872) regulated the opening hours for public houses. Moreover, he tried unsuccessfully to draw the Queen out of her widowhood retirement, and suggested that the Prince of Wales be given a specific job to perform, such as Lord Lieutenant of Ireland.

These reforms did not please everybody and, as a result, the Liberals were defeated at the general election of 1874. Gladstone was forced to resign as prime minister. and as leader of his party, and was succeeded by Disraeli. He now intended to retire from politics and he may well have done so had it not been for the Bulgarian rebellion, when the persecuted Christians rebelled against the Turks in 1875. The inaction of Disraeli against the Turks incensed Gladstone, who wrote a pamphlet entitled *The Bulgarian Horrors* which sold 200,000 copies within a month and re-established him in politics.

In the general election of 1880 he was returned for Midlothian, having toured Scotland on what Victoria condemned as an undignified canvassing campaign. The Conservatives were defeated and once again the Queen was forced to ask Gladstone to become prime minister. However, this second ministry was not as glorious as his first. The problems in Ireland, which he hoped to disunite, were still unresolved, and in 1882 Lord Frederick Cavendish, the new Viceroy, was assassinated in Phoenix Park, Dublin, on the day of his arrival. There was trouble in the Sudan and when General Gordon was killed at Khartoum, the Queen, among others, blamed Gladstone for his death. Gladstone, whose only real achievement was the passing of the third Reform Act (1884), extending the vote to agricultural workers, resigned when the Government was defeated over the budget on 8 June 1885. Gladstone declined the Queen's offer to become an earl and was succeeded by Lord Salisbury. The Salisbury administration was shortlived and on 30 January 1886 Gladstone became premier for the third time.

Gladstone's main interest was still home rule for Ireland and in April 1886 he introduced his Home Rule Bill. This was defeated and Gladstone resigned and was succeeded again by Salisbury. For six years Gladstone was in opposition, becoming prime minister again on 15 August 1892, for the fourth time and at the age of eighty-two. He was still desperate to pacify Ireland and introduced yet another Home Rule Bill. This time it passed through the House of Commons with a majority of 34 votes, but was rejected by 419 votes to 41 by the House of Lords. Gladstone now realised that his task was hopeless and in a final speech to the Commons, he urged the members to fight the House of Lords. On 3 March 1894 he resigned, after sixty-one years in parliament. He retired to Hawarden Castle, his country home in North Wales, where he died on 19 May 1898. His body lay in state for three days in Westminster Hall before he was buried at Westminster Abbey.

Gladstone had been a great man—a good man and a great prime minister. He was fearless, believing that life 'is a great and noble calling, an elevated and lofty destiny' and he lived it to the greater glory of God. His wife, Catherine Glynne, whom he married in July 1839, was equally religious, and together they brought up a Christian family of eight children. Although she was not especially interested in politics, she chose to share his political life and help him in every way. At one point in his career, Gladstone risked his reputation by visiting the streets of Soho and Piccadilly in search of prostitutes whom he hoped to reform by taking them home to his wife for food, shelter and good counsel. Their marriage was an intensely moral and happy one. She sustained him through all his troubles and was at his bedside with their family when he died from cancer of the mouth. Until the end of his life, the Queen had no time for Gladstone; she showed him no thanks for his great service to his country and mankind and she reproved the Prince of Wales for attending his funeral.

Marquis of Salisbury
(Robert Arthur Talbot Gascoyne-Cecil)

Born 3 February 1830
Married Georgina Alderson (5 sons, 1 daughter)
Ministry 1885–6; 1886–92; 1895–1902 (Conservative) –
Queen Victoria, King Edward VII
Died 22 August 1903. Buried at Hatfield, Hertfordshire

It would not have been at all surprising if the Marquis of Salisbury had fallen into complete political obscurity, sandwiched as he was between the ministries of the mighty Gladstone. But it was not his political position which sent him only faintly into posterity, for he was a great prime minister; it was his own self-effacement and shyness. He ruled during Queen Victoria's Golden and Diamond Jubilees and until after her death, and although she did not have the same personal relationship with him that she had with Melbourne and Disraeli, she regarded him as her best prime minister *per se*.

He was the third son of the 2nd Marquis of Salisbury, but his two elder brothers died and he succeeded to the title when his father died in 1868. He was educated at Eton and Christ

Church, Oxford, but his health was not strong enough to stand up to either: his father took him away from Eton when he was fifteen because of bullying by other boys and educated him at home until he went to Oxford. After two years at university his doctor diagnosed 'a complete breakdown of the nervous system' and Lord Robert was sent on a voyage round the world. He viewed his return to England with great horror knowing that he would arrive in time for the London season 'to be bored to death at dinners and parties'. He hated the gay life of a socialite and much preferred to be alone among his books and botanical specimens, or in his laboratory.

When he returned in 1853, Lord Robert entered the House of Commons as Conservative member for Stamford. In July 1866 he became Secretary of State for India in Lord Derby's Government, but resigned in February 1867 in protest against Disraeli's Reform Bill to extend the franchise. Like the Duke of Wellington, he believed implicitly in the ruling classes, and considered political equality 'not merely a folly, but a chimera'. The following year he translated to the House of Lords and began to establish himself as a very capable speaker and parliamentarian. In Disraeli's second ministry of 1874, Salisbury was invited to become Secretary for India again. Despite his intense dislike and distrust of Disraeli, he accepted the post and, after some cutting verbal exchanges, the two men eventually became firm friends. In 1878 Salisbury succeeded Lord Derby as Foreign Secretary and accompanied Disraeli to the Congress of Berlin where his political expertise and 'consummate mastery of detail', as Disraeli described it, played an important part in achieving 'peace with honour' during the Russo-Turkish war (1877–8). When Disraeli died in 1881, Salisbury succeeded him as leader of the Conservatives in the House of Lords.

Salisbury's policies, which included defending the British Empire, opposing home rule for Ireland and a distrust of democratic government, made a favourable impression on the Queen, who asked him to form a ministry of 'strong and able and safe men' following Gladstone's resignation in June 1885. He combined the role of prime minister with the foreign secretaryship, becoming the first man to hold both posts. His minority Government lasted for seven months, his resignation following in January 1886 when the Liberals defeated the Conservatives at the first election to be fought on the new expanded register.

But he became prime minister again when Gladstone's Home Rule for Ireland Bill split the Liberal Party in July 1886 and the Conservatives gained an enormous majority at the ensuing election.

The Liberal Unionists—a group of Liberals who opposed Gladstone's Irish policy—entered into an alliance with Salisbury and his strong second ministry lasted until August 1892. He passed the Local Government Act (1888), which gave the counties greater control of their own affairs, established a department of agriculture with a government minister to head it, and he introduced free education in elementary schools. He resigned in August 1892 after the Liberals had gained a small majority at the general election and Asquith moved a motion of no-confidence in the Salisbury government.

In 1895 he was prime minister for the third time when the Conservatives achieved their first triumph over the Liberals. Gladstone had by now retired, the Liberals were divided, and Salisbury was reigning supreme, loved and revered by the Queen and the people. Combining again the roles of Foreign Secretary and prime minister, he was mainly concerned with protecting the empire. He remained premier until 11 July 1902 when, an exhausted old man, he handed his resignation to Edward VII. His relations with the new King were not as cordial as those with the old Queen and after his resignation he went abroad, missing Edward's coronation. He then retired to Hatfield House, the Hertfordshire stately home of the Salisbury's, where he died on 22 August 1903.

Like Gladstone, Salisbury was a very moral, Christian man, and a devout member of the Church of England. On 11 July 1857, much against his father's will, he married Georgina Alderson, daughter of a High Court judge. She was several years older than he, also deeply religious and highly intellectual, and was able to share with him his interests in theology and politics. Their marriage was a happy, successful one, until her death in 1899.

Earl of Rosebery (Archibald Philip Primrose)

Born 7 May 1847
Married Hannah Rothschild
(2 sons, 2 daughters)
Ministry 1894–5 (Liberal) –
Queen Victoria
Died 21 May 1929. Buried at
Dalmeny

Lord Rosebery never wanted to be prime minister. In fact, he never really wanted to be in politics. He much preferred breeding his racehorses and gambling, and shed his political responsibilities as soon as he decently could. He won the Derby three times—twice while he was prime minister, in 1894 and 1895, making him unique in this respect—and again in 1905.

He was educated at Eton, where he excelled as a classical scholar, and at Christ Church, Oxford, which he left without taking his degree, as he would not part with the racehorse he had bought, and undergraduates were forbidden to own racehorses. Apart from being a sporting man, he was also a literary man and wrote biographies of the two Pitts, Peel and Napoleon.

On 10 May 1878 Lord Rosebery married Hannah Rothschild, only child of the immensely rich Baron Meyer de Rothschild. The wedding caused much consternation among both families, Rosebery's mother grieving that the bride 'had not the faith and hope of Christ', whilst the Jewish community were equally concerned that one of their richest heiresses was marrying a gentile. But the marriage was extremely happy and successful, Hannah taking a great interest in her husband's political career and providing the push that he needed for success.

Rosebery took his seat in the House of Lords in 1868 and joined Gladstone's Liberals. In 1881, during Gladstone's second administration, he became Under-secretary at the Home Office with responsibility for Scotland, but resigned two years later and went with his wife to Australia. During this trip, which enhanced his imperialism, he created the term 'Commonwealth of Nations' when he referred to the Empire as such during a speech in

Adelaide: '. . . there is no need for any nation, however great, leaving the Empire, because the Empire is a Commonwealth of Nations.'

When he returned to England he became Lord Privy Seal, then Foreign Secretary in Gladstone's third administration, and in 1888 Chairman of the newly formed London County Council. In 1890 his wife died suddenly of typhoid and Rosebery, distraught with grief, vanished into personal solitude. When Gladstone returned to office for the fourth time in 1892 he tried in vain to persuade Rosebery to return as Foreign Secretary. At last the Queen sent the Prince of Wales to force Rosebery out of his decline, and dutifully, but reluctantly, he accepted. Following Gladstone's resignation in 1894 the Queen, using her prerogative, summoned Rosebery to succeed him. Rosebery, still reluctant, but knowing it to be his duty, accepted and hoped that the Cabinet would give him their 'cordial co-operation'. But they did not. They were divided over imperialism and various home issues, and the House of Lords was hostile to all Liberal legislation. Consequently, Rosebery's task was difficult and his ministry achieved few results.

Rosebery found it difficult to control the Commons from his position in the House of Lords, and when a vote of censure was taken against Campbell-Bannerman, his Secretary of State for War, for allegedly failing to ensure that the Army was adequately supplied with cordite, Rosebery gladly found a way out. On 23 June 1895, after fifteen months as premier, he handed his resignation to the Queen. A year later he relinquished the leadership of the Liberals, and took an independent stand. He died on 21 May 1929 and is buried at Dalmeny.

Rosebery might well have been one of the greatest prime ministers, but his profound intelligence and political talent were never exploited to the full. He suffered severely from insomnia and was ravaged by indecision. He was a politically lonely man, who needed the strength and support of his wife and, when she died, he was helpless. Some years later he revealed that he had always hated politics, which he had drifted into accidentally, and that when he found himself 'in this evil-smelling bog I was always trying to extricate myself. That is the secret of what people used to call my lost opportunities, and so forth'.

Arthur James Balfour

Born 25 July 1848
Unmarried
Ministry 1902–5 (Conservative)
– King Edward VII
Died 19 March 1930. Buried at
Whittinghame, E. Lothian

Arthur Balfour was the first bachelor prime minister since the Younger Pitt, a century before him. He was the natural political heir of his uncle, Lord Salisbury, who had trained him in politics, so it was not surprising that he took over the premiership from his uncle on his retirement in 1902.

An aesthete, interested in philosophy, religion, poetry and music, he loathed the usual sporting pursuits of the aristocrat and consequently acquired the nickname 'Pretty Fanny' whilst at Cambridge. On leaving university, his real hope was to become a philosopher but his mother reminded him of his social status and his duty to society. Despite his political career, however, he became a philosopher, proving his ability by writing several works, including *A Defence of Philosophic Doubt, The Foundations of Belief*, and *Theism and Humanism*, and he was accepted professionally by other philosophers.

Balfour entered Parliament in 1874 as Conservative member for Hertford. Four years later he became private secretary to Salisbury, then Foreign Secretary in Disraeli's government, and accompanied them both to the Congress of Berlin. This was the beginning of his close association with his uncle—an association which was to be compared with that of their great Elizabethan ancestors, Lord Burghley and his son Robert Cecil, who together served their Queen and country three centuries earlier.

Whilst in opposition during Gladstone's second ministry Balfour headed a ginger-group (known as the Fourth Party since they stood aloof from the Conservatives, Liberals and Irish Nationalists), which brought down the Government in 1885 with a motion opposing Gladstone's Home Rule for Ireland Bill.

Balfour then became Secretary for Scotland in Salisbury's first ministry, and in 1887 Secretary for Ireland in Salisbury's second ministry. This appointment sent the political world, especially in Ireland, into hysterical incredulity. 'Pretty Fanny', the beautiful, willowy child of the muses—what could he do within the inflammable walls of Dublin? Home rule was one of the country's all-consuming questions and the Irish Secretaryship was one of the toughest and most important Cabinet posts of that time. But Salisbury knew his nephew. With his brilliant wit, equable temper, and fearless courage, Balfour established himself in Ireland, fighting off the personal abuse and proving himself to be one of the finest Secretaries of all time. He stayed in Dublin until 1891, during which time he was responsible for the Land Purchase Act (1881) and the Congested District Act. These, together with his land development and drainage schemes, gave the Irish a chance to prosper and so brought about a quiescence which lasted for almost twenty years. In 1891 he became First Lord of the Treasury and Leader of the House of Commons until the fall of Salisbury's ministry in 1892. He held the posts again in Salisbury's third administration of 1895, until he became prime minister in 1902 on Salisbury's retirement.

Education of the people, and the defence of Britain and her empire were his main concerns. He thought that there was 'no more serious waste than the waste of brains and intellect'. And Britain's incompetent management of the South African War horrified him. He immediately pushed through his Education Act (1902) which abolished school boards and made local authorities responsible for elementary education, and set up the Committee for Imperial Defence to ensure that Britain was prepared for any future war.

But his ministry was not entirely happy. He and the King were not fond of each other; his Cabinet was split between the new Tariff Reformers under Joseph Chamberlain, the Colonial Secretary, and the Free Traders under Chancellor Charles Ritchie, and, furthermore, agitation was growing in the country over the Education Act, particularly among Non-conformists who objected to paying rates to support Church of England schools. With the dawn of the Edwardian era came the dawn of a new liberalism. Balfour, suffering defeats in the lobbies and at by-elections, resigned in December 1905. At the general election that followed, the Tory Government was swept away in a crushing defeat by the Liberals, and Henry Campbell-Bannerman became prime minister. Balfour himself was overwhelmingly defeated in his Manchester constituency, but was returned as member for the City of London in a by-election shortly afterwards, and resumed the Conservative Party leadership until he resigned in 1911.

In 1915 he became First Lord of the Admiralty in Asquith's coalition ministry. Later, on 2 November 1917, whilst he was Foreign Secretary in Lloyd George's administration, he signed the 'Balfour Declaration'—a cabinet decision to establish a 'national home for the Jewish people' in Palestine. He became *Trouble ever since* Lord President of the Council from 1919–22 under Lloyd George and then from 1925–9 in Baldwin's second administration. He resigned with the fall of the Baldwin Government in May 1929 and retired to his brother's home in Woking, Surrey. He died on 19 March 1930 and is buried, as he had requested, at his birthplace of Whittinghame, in East Lothian, Scotland.

Balfour, created an earl in 1922, was very rich, handsome and eligible. Women were attracted to him and he delighted in their company. With his easy wit, brilliant conversation and philosophical outlook he was welcome in the drawing-rooms of London and the stately homes of the country. But he never married. His first love, Mary Lyttleton, the niece of Mrs Gladstone, died suddenly of typhoid in March 1875, and Balfour was to show his sensitivity by weeping in public at her funeral. His great love affair with Lord Elcho's wife, Mary, endured for many years.

As well as being a philosopher and writer, Balfour was also a scientist and foresaw the application of science to industry. Like his uncle, he was deeply religious, with a life-long belief in a personal God to whom men may pray. Although not a spiritualist, he was interested in spiritualism and was a founder member, and then president, of the Society for Psychical Research.

Sir Henry Campbell-Bannerman

Born 7 September 1836
Married Charlotte Bruce (no
children)
Ministry 1905–8 (Liberal) –
King Edward VII
Died 22 April 1908. Buried at
Meigle, Strathmore

Henry Campbell-Bannerman was one of the most successful, if not so well known, of British prime ministers. He was a sensible, genial politician, afraid of no man and nothing and devoted his whole life to the Liberal cause. He was a firm believer in free trade, home rule for Ireland and the improvement of social conditions. Rich, generous and somewhat a dandy, he and his wife entertained lavishly in their London and country homes and every autumn, come what may, they spent six weeks at the German spa town of Marienbad. He was devoted to his wife and consulted her about all his affairs.

Although he was the thirty-fourth man to hold office as prime minister since Robert Walpole established the position in April 1721, Campbell-Bannerman was the first to be officially recognised as such. As the holder of an official status, the prime minister now ranked fourth in the order of precedence—after royalty, the Archbishops of Canterbury and York, and the Lord Chancellor.

Sir Henry, or CB as he was always known, was the youngest son of Sir James Campbell, a Scottish businessman and Lord Provost of Glasgow, and was educated at Glasgow High School and Glasgow and Cambridge universities. In 1868, after ten years in the family business, he entered the House of Commons as MP for Stirling Burghs. Gladstone was prime minister and before long he recognised his fellow canny Scot's business acumen and appointed him Financial Secretary at the War Office. That same year, Sir Henry's maternal uncle died and left him some property provided he used his name of Bannerman. And so Henry

Campbell became Henry Campbell-Bannerman.

He was out of office during Disraeli's second administration, but returned when Gladstone became prime minister again, and became Secretary of State for War in 1886. An advocate of home rule—for any nationality—he followed Gladstone when the Liberals split in 1886 over the Home Rule for Ireland Bill. In 1892 he became Secretary of State for War again under Gladstone and continued under Rosebery until 1895, when a vote of censure against him for allegedly failing to see that the army was adequately supplied with cordite, compelled him and Rosebery's Government to resign—but not before CB had forced the resignation of the Duke of Cambridge, Queen Victoria's cousin, as Commander-in-Chief of the Army.

But everyone was not against CB—he had the sympathy of the army and Queen Victoria, who held him in high esteem, made him a Knight of the Bath. Four years later he became leader of the Liberals. Salisbury was now prime minister of his Conservative administration, and when the South African War broke out on 11 October 1899 the Liberal Party once again divided itself, this time between the Liberal Imperialists, headed by Asquith, who supported the war, and those who denounced it, headed by Campbell-Bannerman and Lloyd George. During one of his anti-war speeches, CB called Kitchener's scorched-earth policy[26] 'methods of barbarism'. Although this remark caused an outcry in the House and in the country, he refused to withdraw it. This strong, highly principled character behind the genial façade successfully united the Liberal Party when the war was over, and when Balfour resigned in December 1905, Edward VII summoned CB to Buckingham Palace and asked him to form a ministry.

Campbell-Bannerman was almost seventy and his health was failing, so it was hoped that he would accept a peerage and leave the Commons leadership to Asquith. This plan had been connived by Asquith and other leading Liberals with the King's private secretary. But the sorely offended CB, backed by his wife, refused the peerage. He formed his administration, one of the strongest and most efficient ever, and led it to a resounding victory over the Conservatives in the election of January 1906. His administration represented Liberals of all opinions: the Imperialist Asquith as Chancellor and Sir Edward Grey as Foreign Secretary; the Radical Lloyd George as President of the Board of Trade; the Labour leader, John Burns as President of the Local Government Board; and the Free Trade Conservative defector, Winston Churchill as Under-secretary of State for the Colonies. CB, showing great leadership and tenacity, was now highly respected by the King, Parliament and the country.

The following August Lady Campbell-Bannerman died from a stroke, leaving CB desolate and heartbroken. 'Alone in the world . . .' he carried on, 'with God's help, as she would have had me go on . . ..' for another eighteen months, during which time he passed the Trade Disputes Act (1906) and restored self-government to the defeated Boer republics of Transvaal and Orange Free State. His government's Education Bill was defeated by the Lords, which brought the two Houses into conflict. CB's health deteriorated, until on 12 February 1908, heart trouble forced him to take to his bed at No. 10 Downing Street. Too ill to be moved, he remained there until he died on 22 April 1908, having resigned a few weeks earlier on 3 April.

Herbert Henry Asquith

Born 12 September 1852
Married (1) Helen Melland (4
sons, 1 daughter); (2) Margot
Tennant (1 son, 1 daughter)
Ministry 1908–16 (Liberal) –
Kings Edward VII, George V
Died 15 February 1928. Buried
at Sutton Courtenay

Mr Asquith, as he was always called, was prime minister during one of the most difficult and changing periods in history. And he gave the people their real chance—with his Parliament Act, when he used his famous words 'Wait and See', and the beginnings of the Welfare State. When he succeeded to the premiership, he became the first prime minister to receive the seals of office on foreign soil—in Biarritz, where the King was on holiday.

Asquith was a Liberal of Gladstonian persuasion, believing in free trade, home rule for Ireland and social reform. The second

84

son of a Yorkshire wool merchant, he was educated at the City of London School and Balliol College, Oxford, where he distinguished himself as a classical scholar and debater; he then entered Lincoln's Inn and was called to the Bar. Clearly an academic or legal path laid itself before him, but Asquith had decided on a political career and at the general election of 1886 he was returned as Liberal candidate for East Fife.

His keen intellect and administrative ability soon became apparent to Gladstone who appointed him Home Secretary in his fourth administration in 1892. Asquith continued in the post during Rosebery's administration, and proved himself one of the most brilliant home secretaries of all times. For ten years from 1895, during the Conservative administrations of Salisbury and Balfour, he was out of office and returned to his barrister's practice—an unprecented step for a member of the Cabinet. While in opposition Asquith followed Joseph Chamberlain, the Colonial Secretary, round the country, making speeches contrary to Chamberlain's imperial-preference tariff reform appeals to the people. It was his eloquence and skill as an advocate which roused the country to stay with free trade and vote against Chamberlain's policy.

When the Liberals were swept back to power with their massive majority in the 1905 general election, Asquith became Chancellor of the Exchequer under Campbell-Bannerman. Social reform was the keynote of Liberal policy and Asquith set about its implementation. Among his achievements were the imposition of a higher rate of tax on unearned income, and the provision for old age pensions—5s. 0d (25p) a week to everyone over seventy years of age whose income did not exceed 10s. 0d (50p) a week. By 1908 Asquith had succeeded to the premiership following Campbell-Bannerman's death, and the budget covering pensions was introduced by the new Chancellor, Lloyd George. Presiding over a brilliant Cabinet, Asquith took up the fight against the House of Lords—an issue which had defeated Gladstone.

The Lords, consisting mainly of Tories, were always obstructive to Liberal policy, rejecting bill after bill, and in 1909 they rejected Lloyd George's People's Budget. This was a money bill and although Britain had no written constitution it had been generally accepted for more than two hundred years that the Lords did not reject money bills—but the Lords claimed that this budget was more than a money bill.

Asquith took up the gauntlet, dissolved Parliament and in January 1910 the country went to the polls in the People versus the Lords election. The Liberals were returned, but with only a slight majority over the Conservatives. Asquith now had to depend upon the Labour and Irish members to enable him to remain prime minister. The Irish members pledged their support if Asquith would introduce a bill to prevent the Lords' veto and so give home rule for Ireland a better chance of acceptance. Asquith agreed to the bargain and when asked how he could accomplish this, he remarked cryptically, 'Wait and see'. (This was the only occasion these famous words were used by Asquith, although the phrase has come to be associated with his name because the newspapers threw it back at him when they accused him of vacillating during World War I.)

In April 1910 he introduced the Parliament Bill which stated that the Lords could not interfere with money bills; that any other bill which had passed through the Commons in three successive years, even if rejected by the Lords, would automatically become law; and that a parliamentary term should be reduced from seven to five years. Early in May Edward VII had died so Asquith appealed to the new King, George V, to create new peers if the Parliament Bill did not pass through the Lords —reminiscent of Earl Grey's appeal to William IV for his Reform Bill in 1832. The king's guarantee to create 250 Liberal peers to ensure its passage proved unnecessary, however, and the bill was finally passed by the Lords in August 1911.

The Parliament Act diminished the Lords' veto considerably since they would now be able to hold up a bill for only two years. Asquith consequently introduced his Home Rule for Ireland Bill, but by 1914 this had passed twice through the Commons and had twice been rejected by the Lords. It did not have an easy passage—the Ulstermen did not want home rule and, with the support of Sir Edward Carson, their leader at Westminster, and Bonar Law, the leader of the Conservatives, they were prepared to take up arms against the bill. Asquith's task was not an easy one. Besides the Ireland Bill, Women's suffrage was rearing its head, and there were strikes by miners and railwaymen. But all this was overshadowed by the outbreak of war with Germany on 4 August 1914, which was to cause the downfall of Asquith. Yet it was mainly thanks to his leadership that the country entered the war as a united people.

In May 1915 Asquith formed a coalition government which included Balfour, Bonar Law, Carson and Joseph Chamberlain's son, Austen, for the Conservative Party, and the Labour supporter Arthur Henderson; Lord Kitchener was War Minister and Lloyd George Minister for Munitions. But the coalition was not successful and the Government soon became unpopular. The war, which was claiming heavy casualties, was having no apparent success. Asquith was accused of procrastination and of giving more importance to his own self-interests than to the war; the newspapers started to campaign against him, using his cryptic remark of five years before, 'wait and see', as a weapon, and he was vilified and satirised in the press and in the music halls.

Events worsened in 1916, which was to become a fateful year for Asquith. At Easter there was the Sinn Fein rising in Dublin, when the Irish Republicans declared their independence; in June Lord Kitchener was drowned when HMS *Hampshire*, in which he was travelling to Russia, struck a mine; and, worst of all for Asquith personally, his eldest son was among the thousands of young men killed at the battle of the Somme in July. Asquith was griefstricken. But this did not prevent the campaign against him from intensifying. Lloyd George had replaced Kitchener as War Minister, much to the disgust of Mrs Asquith, who saw the new appointment as the beginning of the end for Asquith. In her diary she wrote: 'We are out. It can only be a question of time now before we have to leave Downing Street.'

Lloyd George, who worked ceaselessly putting his country's needs before his own, became increasingly popular with the Government and the people. At the beginning of December, he suggested that a small war committee should be appointed to actively direct the war, with the prime minister, while not a member of the committee, retaining supreme control of war policy. Asquith agreed to the suggestion until *The Times* attacked him, implying that he was taking a subordinate position in his own government and praising Lloyd George's competence. Asquith then rejected the suggestion, and Lloyd George, who said that he could not stay in a Government with whose delaying policy he disagreed, resigned. Asquith's Liberal colleagues pledged their support, but the Conservatives rallied round Lloyd George, believing that the prime minister should resign. This he did on 5 December 1916. No doubt he thought Bonar Law and

Lloyd George would be asked to form ministries and would fail, and that he would be returned with more power and prestige. But Bonar Law and his colleagues chose to serve under Lloyd George who became prime minister on 7 December.

Asquith declined the King's offer of the Garter and also refused to serve under Lloyd George. He remained out of office, gradually losing support, until, in the election of 1918, he lost his seat at East Fife after thirty-two years. Only twenty-six Asquithian Liberals were returned to the Commons and Asquith was deeply hurt. He was now shunned by his old supporters and refused a public platform.

Then in a by-election at Paisley in 1920, he was returned as an Independent Liberal and made a triumphant return to the Commons. But Asquith was disappointed with the breed of new members he found there—they seemed to be hard-faced business-men who had feathered their nests during the war.

After the fall of Lloyd George's government in 1922, Asquith reunited the Liberal Party once more under his leadership, but the rift between him and Lloyd George did not heal. With the fall of Bonar Law's Conservative Government in 1924, the Liberals held the balance between Labour and Conservative. Asquith maintaining that Labour must be given a chance some-time, gave them that chance, even though it was to strangle the Liberal Party, and Ramsay MacDonald became prime minister of the first ever Labour government in 1924. But Macdonald's Government toppled by the end of the year, and in the ensuing election Asquith lost his seat at Paisley in a straight fight with Labour. He was now seventy-two and the prospects of returning to Parliament were remote. King George offered him a peerage and persuaded him to return to Westminster by stressing his importance to the nation. Although Asquith took his seat in the House of Lords as Earl of Oxford and Asquith in December 1924, he was not happy there, spending most of his time instead at his country house at Sutton Courtenay, a Thameside village in Berkshire. In 1927 he had a stroke and died on 15 February 1928. With Asquith died 'the last of the Romans', those great classical scholars who became politicians.

Asquith had been prime minister longer than anyone since Lord Liverpool a century earlier. And while he was changing the face of the country his wife was changing the face of No. 10 Downing Street. His first wife, Helen Melland, died of typhoid in August 1891. Asquith had fallen in love with her when he was eighteen, and she fifteen, and their fourteen years of marriage had been very successful and happy. Then in 1894, when he was forty-one and the father of five children, he married the twenty-six-year-old socialite, Margot Tennant, daughter of the rich financier baronet, Sir Charles Tennant. She was an extrovert, gay and vital and a little racy.

While resident at Downing Street they entertained a vast and talented circle of writers, artists and distinguished people outside politics. Asquith had much contact with people, not only in his own social set, but in the ordinary walks of life. But much of his behaviour left him open to criticism. He preferred an intellectual life to a sporting one, and what he liked most of all was a game of bridge, and would see no wrong in spending weekends away in the country even during the stormy days of the war. He was very popular among his own circles, but outwardly he appeared a cold, grave resolute man. As an orator he ranked among the greatest.

David Lloyd George

Born 17 January 1863
Married (1) Margaret Owen (2 sons, 3 daughters); (2) Frances Stevenson (1 daughter before marriage)
Ministry 1916–22 (Liberal) – King George V
Died 26 March 1945. Buried at Llanystumdwy, Wales

Some people loved him, others loathed him—but none could ever ignore him. That was David Lloyd George, the fiery little Welshman who rose from the lowly cobbler's smithy in Caernarvonshire to the highest office in the land.

Lloyd George, who succeeded Mr Asquith as prime minister, was a legend in his own lifetime. He hated oppression, of which he had seen plenty, and detested rich landowners, who to him were synonymous with oppression, and from the moment he

89

entered Parliament he made himself heard in his ceaseless fight against them both.

Although his origins were humble, they were certainly not mean. His father, William George, was a school master in Manchester, where David and his elder sister were born. When David was three months old his father returned to his native Pembrokeshire where he died, a year later, and David's mother took her family to Llanystumdwy, a village near Criccieth in Caernarvonshire, to live with her brother, Richard Lloyd, a cobbler who ran the family shoemaking business. It was in this corner of Wales that David Lloyd George grew up. It was here that he learned that people were not equal—that there were the oppressed and the oppressors, and it was here that he determined to succeed and fight for the underdog.

His first fight for justice was at the village school he attended from the age of four. This was an anglican school, but David was a non-conformist and fought against being taught the anglican faith. He won his fight, but this did not jeopardise his chances at school. He was a clever boy, with a phenomenal memory and excelled at everything, particularly maths, public speaking and debating. At the school leaving age of twelve, he had decided to become a lawyer, but the entrance examinations for legal training included Latin and French. David knew neither language, so the headmaster agreed to let him remain at school for another year so that he could teach him Latin. Even the headmaster did not know French, so when David left school his Uncle Richard, who besides being the cobbler, was a lay preacher, and an eager supporter of the Liberal Party, decided to teach David himself. He did not know French himself but he was a well-read eloquent man, and every night for a year he and David groped their way through a French grammar and dictionary, in what seemed an impossible task. But to them nothing was impossible, and their task accomplished, David passed the Law Society examination and in 1879 was articled to a firm of solicitors in Portmadoc where he worked under a prominent local Liberal who encouraged him to participate in political activities. David already had a grounding in politics, having participated in the debates of local Liberals in his uncle's smithy, and he now joined the Portmadoc Debating Society, spoke in various chapels, contributed to local newspapers, and spoke well in court.

In 1883 he passed his final examinations as a lawyer, and set up practice from a room in his family house in Criccieth, winning every case he undertook, most of which were against landlords. In 1890 he was invited to stand as Liberal candidate at the by-election in Caernarvon and, unable to resist the challenge on learning that his opponent in this safe Tory seat was the landlord of his own village, he accepted. He won the seat and, at the age of twenty-seven, entered Parliament.

Outside his own little Welsh circle he was unknown. But not for long. The Liberals were in opposition, and Lloyd George soon earned himself the title of 'the Welsh Wizard' when he fired his wit and vitriolic ridicule at the Tory squires he loathed so much. Lord Salisbury's Government began to respect, albeit detest, the fiery Welshman and few wanted to encounter him in debate.

With the outbreak of the Boer War, Lloyd George established his name in politics forever. He opposed the war, thinking it immoral for Britain to bully a small state like the Transvaal on behalf of a few avaricious goldminers with whom he was totally unsympathetic. He became immensely unpopular when he slated Joseph Chamberlain, the Colonial Secretary, who had instigated the war and who, with the country's support, approved of it. He toured the country addressing meetings and often swayed a hostile audience to his way of thinking. But he went too far when he tried to address a meeting in Chamberlain's constituency of Birmingham. A riot broke out and mobs devastated the town hall where he was to speak. Death and injury resulted and Lloyd George was forced to escape disguised as a policeman. By the war's end in 1902, Lloyd George was well and truly detested in the country, but he was also well and truly known—and that was what he wanted. Balfour, now Prime Minister, admitted that Lloyd George was an eminent politician whose fearlessness and eloquence could not be denied.

When the Liberals came to power in 1906, Lloyd George was appointed President of the Board of Trade, and among his achievements was the establishment of the Port of London Authority. Further, he used his powers of persuasion to calm the unrest in industry and avert strikes by dockers and railway-men. His ability as a statesman was now generally recognised and the press extolled his sober qualities, genius and ability. Asquith also respected him and, on assuming the premiership, appointed

Lloyd George as his Chancellor of the Exchequer.

Now he was at last in a position to really help the deprived poverty stricken. His first task was to introduce Asquith's budget, giving pensions to those over the age of seventy. His own People's Budget the following year was what he called a war budget—waging war on poverty. He planned to spend millions of pounds of public money on old age pensions, roads, labour exchanges, national parks, and various other social reforms; he also planned to build new battleships, fearing that the German Navy was stronger than Britain's. To pay for all this he intended to bleed the rich he detested by taxing land, increasing death duties and introducing super-tax. This caused an outcry in both Commons and Lords, but Lloyd George declared it was a 'war budget to raise money to wage implacable warfare against poverty and squalidness.' A Budget Protest League was formed by the Tories, and Lloyd George responded with vitriolic attacks on landowners and dukes in public houses in the East End of London. One of his speeches, in which he thundered: 'Who is going to rule the country? The King and the peers, or the King and the people?' prompted a letter from George V to Asquith asking that the King's name be left out of politics.

The budget, which was the first money bill to be rejected by the Lords for over two hundred years, had a very stormy passage but was eventually passed on 28 April 1910. In 1911 the Parliament Act was passed, which considerably reduced the Lords' veto (see page 86).

Lloyd George's National Insurance Bill, making insurance against sickness and unemployment compulsory for manual workers between the ages of sixteen and seventy, also suffered a stormy passage in the hands of the moneyed classes, but the working classes supported him, and the bill became law in 1912. Lloyd George was now recognised as the most radical of Liberals and a great social reformer; it can be said that he firmly established the welfare state begun by Asquith with the introduction of old age pensions in 1908.

On 4 August 1914, Britain declared war on Germany, and Lloyd George determined from the start that Britain should be the victor. He immediately tackled Britain's financial arrangements, closing the Stock Exchange to stop panic selling of shares, replacing gold sovereigns with Treasury notes and launching various schemes to bring in money to fight the war. Believing the War Office could not cope with the supply of ammunition to the soldiers in the trenches in France, Lloyd George persuaded Asquith to let him set up and head a munitions committee, and a few weeks later, when Asquith formed his Coalition, Lloyd George left the Treasury and became the first Minister for Munitions.

Lloyd George's dynamic and untiring leadership spurred on 25,000 workers in what became the world's largest industrial concern. Anyone and anything that could be used for making munitions was used; he persuaded the trade unions to abandon their demarcation lines so that the effort would not be held up and, for the first time, women were able to offer their services. The result was that before long the soldiers in the trenches were getting all the ammunition they needed.

Lloyd George headed the Munitions Ministry for thirteen months until, reluctantly, he became War Minister following the death of Lord Kitchener, who was drowned when HMS *Hampshire* hit a mine and was sunk whilst on its way to Russia. For many months Lloyd George had disapproved of the way the war was being directed and although he admired Asquith's intelligence and ability as a prime minister in peacetime, he did not admire his strength as a leader in wartime and believed that the war was being lost on his account. After the battle of the Somme, when 57,000 men were killed on the first day and thousands more, including Asquith's eldest son, perished in the ensuing months, Lloyd George could approve of Asquith's war policy no longer. He suggested that he, Lloyd George, should head a small war committee to direct the war but that Asquith, although retaining supreme control of war policy, would not be a member.

Asquith agreed to the proposal but was soon attacked by the press. *The Times* accused him of taking a subordinate post in his own Cabinet but at the same time praised Lloyd George. Asquith then withdrew his agreement and Lloyd George resigned on the grounds that he disapproved of the Government's policies. Believing no doubt that he would be asked to form another administration, Asquith also resigned. The King however immediately sent for Bonar Law, who declined as he, together with his Conservative colleagues and a number of Liberals, believed that Lloyd George was the man to serve the country as premier. So, on 7 December 1916 Lloyd George became the first Welsh prime minister.

Lloyd George knew what he wanted, and he proved to be the finest war leader since Pitt the Elder, a century and a half earlier. He set up a small War Cabinet consisting of himself, Bonar Law, Lords Curzon and Milner, and Arthur Henderson. He knew his task was not an easy one. Britain was having little success in the war: the Germans had launched a U-boat offensive to sink all ships heading for Britain, and more than 500,000 tons of shipping were lost each month, while at home food supplies were decreasing. Undeterred, Lloyd George ordered the Admiralty to arrange for merchant ships to sail in convoys escorted by warships. He dismissed the First Lord of the Admiralty for his lack of co-operation in the scheme and ordered the Admiralty to make it work. Success was achieved with the result that losses of merchant ships fell to less than 1 per cent.

Lloyd George also set up Ministries of Food, Shipping, Pensions, Air and Labour as well as introducing National Service in the effort to win the war.

He then turned his attention to army tactics, of which he had long disapproved. For three years thousands of British soldiers had been stuck in the trenches in France getting nowhere, except to their death, and Lloyd George thought they could be better used elsewhere. But this was not the view of Douglas Haig, British Commander-in-Chief on the Western Front, an orthodox and unimaginative professional soldier, whose popularity made it impossible for Lloyd George to dismiss him. He argued that, as Britain and France had more men than Germany, they could afford to wait and hope to exhaust the Germans. He put his plan to the test at the battle of Passchendaele in Flanders which, with the loss of 400,000 men, achieved no positive advance. Still unable to dismiss Haig, Lloyd George limited his power by arranging with the French Prime Minister for Marshal Foch to be Supreme Commander of the allied armies in France.

The year 1917 had not been a good one. Besides Passchendaele the Bolshevik Revolution had caused the collapse of Russia who had made peace with Germany, enabling that country to reinforce the Western Front with troops. Foreseeing the attack, Lloyd George urged President Wilson of America, who had just entered the war, to send his troops across the Atlantic as fast as possible, and British ships were sent to transport them. When in March 1918 the Germans launched their attack a desperate battle for victory ensured with enormous casualties on both sides.

In July, the arrival in France of 300,000 Americans proved invaluable, and news that the allied force had captured Bulgaria together with defeats in France, convinced the Germans of the inevitability of defeat. On 9 November the Kaiser abdicated and escaped to Holland. At 11 am on 11 November 1918 Germany surrendered and the war came to an end.

In the House of Commons that afternoon, Lloyd George told the members:

At eleven o'clock this morning came to an end the cruellest and most terrible war that has ever scourged mankind. I hope we may say that thus, this fateful morning, came to an end all wars. This is no time for words. Our hearts are too full of gratitude to which no tongue can give adequate expression. I will, therefore, move 'That this House do immediately adjourn until this time tomorrow, and that we proceed, as a House of Commons, to St Margaret's to give humble and reverent thanks for the deliverance of the world from its great peril.'

Then he led the Members across the road to the church.

The country was jubilant at the victory, and Lloyd George was acclaimed as the man who had won the war. But at the same time the people were demanding that the Kaiser should be hanged and Germany punished so forcibly that she could never again start a war. Nine million men, one million of whom were British, and even more French, had been killed, and thirty million wounded in that war which had cost Britain and her allies £24,000 million.

Lloyd George was now at the peak of his fame. The King conferred on him the Order of Merit, France gave him the Legion of Honour, and other countries, universities and cities bestowed upon him their highest awards.

In the post-war general election at the end of 1918 the Lloyd George–Bonar Law coalition won an overwhelming victory, although the larger part went to Bonar Law's Conservatives. This election was the first in which women could vote, for under the Representation of the People Act (1918), women over thirty, who were either householders or the wives of householders, were given the franchise.

With the arrival of peace Lloyd George had now to help in the rebuilding of Europe. On 28 June 1919, with Woodrow Wilson, the American President, and Prime Ministers

Clemenceau of France, and Orlando of Italy, he signed the Treaty of Versailles, which established the League of Nations[28] and forced Germany to make reparations to Europe. Affairs at home were not so easily settled, however, and even the little Welsh Wizard became despondent. There was still trouble in Ireland with the rebellion of Sinn Feiners, and Lloyd George reluctantly signed an agreement between Britain and Ireland by which Southern Ireland became a free state on 6 December 1921. In Britain hundreds of workers were unemployed and there was widespread depression and strikes in industry. Lloyd George's popularity faded as the workers found he could not fulfil his promises of a 'land fit for heroes to live in'.

In 1922 the Conservatives decided to fight the general election alone without a coalition. Lloyd George was denounced as a war monger when war with Kemal Ataturk's Turkey looked imminent. There was no war, and indeed Lloyd George had been instrumental in preventing it. But it was considered he had served his purpose and was no longer useful. On 19 October 1922 he went to Buckingham Palace and handed his resignation to King George V. The King was genuinely sorry to see him go and noted in his diary 'some day he will be prime minister again'. But Lloyd George never held office again.

With the fall of the coalition, the Liberal Party collapsed and was superseded by the Labour Party. Lloyd George continued to sit in the Commons and, had he not suffered ill-health, he might have been included in Ramsay MacDonald's National Government of 1931. One of his last acts was to help bring about the fall of Neville Chamberlain in 1940, whom he bitterly attacked over the failure of the expedition to Norway. Chamberlain was replaced by Churchill who offered Lloyd George a place in his Cabinet, but the old man was now too weary. He made his last speech in the Commons on 11 June 1942.

In 1944 he was created Earl Lloyd-George of Dwyfor. On 26 March 1945, after fifty-five years in Parliament, he died at the age of eighty-two—a grand old man who had helped to shape the structure of present-day Britain. He is buried in a grave he chose for himself on the bank of the River Dwyfor.

Lloyd George's personal life was almost as colourful as his professional life, but sensibly he kept it private. He was an attractive man, brilliantly intelligent, with a burning passion to help others and see justice done. With his soft musical voice and poetic soul, he was attracted by women, who in turn were attracted to him. His love affairs were numerous and when his wife berated him over these, he told her she should accept this facet of his nature and make allowances for the 'waywardness and wildness of a man of my type'. Early in his marriage he met and fell in love with Frances Stevenson, a young school teacher who became his private secretary. Their love affair endured to the end of Lloyd George's life and by her he had one daughter. His first wife, by whom he had five children, died in 1941, and Lloyd George and Frances married two years later. He then took her back to his beloved Wales where they spent the rest of their days.

Andrew Bonar Law

Born 16 September 1858
Married Annie Pitcairn Robley
(4 sons, 2 daughters)
Ministry 1922–3 (Conservative)
– King George V
Died 30 October 1923. Buried
in Westminster Abbey

Gentle and unassuming, Bonar Law was the direct opposite of the colourful, ebullient Lloyd George whom he succeeded as prime minister; yet the two men were great friends and worked as one of the finest political partnerships in history.

The son of an expatriate Ulsterman, Andrew Bonar Law was born in New Brunswick, Canada, where his father, the Reverend James Law was minister of the Free Church of Scotland. His mother died when he was two years old and Bonar was brought up by his maternal aunt in the frugal surroundings of his father's clerical home. To supplement his stipend, the Reverend Law worked a smallholding, where Bonar toiled when he returned each day from the village school. Life was hard for the boy, but when he was twelve his father remarried and his aunt took

97

him to Scotland, the land of his forefathers. There in Glasgow life was comfortable, for Bonar lived with his mother's cousins who were rich merchant bankers. When he left school he went into the family's merchant bank and, to further his education, went to night school at Glasgow University; he read avidly developing an interest in politics as a result of his reading, and joined the Glasgow Parliamentary Debating Society.

In 1885, when he was twenty-seven, the ageing cousins sold the family bank and Bonar, who had been well provided for, took up a partnership in industry. Although he was now rich his life did not change much, for he was not a gregarious man. His outdoor interests were golf and tennis, his indoor pleasures were chess, whist and bridge. He did not drink, although he smoked incessantly. He was a dour, pessimistic man, who confessed to Lloyd George years later that he had no interest in music, scenery, or women. Nevertheless, in 1891, he married Annie Pitcairn Robley, a shipbroker's daughter. Law was by now a very successful businessman with a predilection for facts and figures and the ability and memory to put them to good use. Very soon his old cousins died, leaving him legacies of £60,000. Now financially independent, he decided to go into politics, and in 1900 was elected Conservative member for Blackfriars, Glasgow.

When he entered Parliament, he found the tightly-knit coterie of the Salisbury-Balfour aristocrats rather awesome and joined Joseph Chamberlain, an ordinary man like himself, whose Tariff Reform campaign he supported with well prepared arguments. He rapidly gained a reputation as an honest, hard-hitting, fearless politician, and in Balfour's administration of 1902 he became Parliamentary Secretary to the Board of Trade.

He was defeated in the 1906 election by the Labour candidate, George Barnes, but a few months later was returned at a by-election at Dulwich. Steadily he improved his political image, and in the turmoil of 1909, when Asquith was fighting the House of Lords, Law came to the fore, assailing Lloyd George's budget as 'pure and unadulterated socialism', and upholding the House of Lords' veto. Then the first tragedy of his life struck— his wife died suddenly, leaving him desolate and intent on giving up politics for ever. But he was persuaded to carry on, with the help of his sister to care for him and his children. Quietly, but forcefully, he plodded on, and when Balfour resigned the Party

Leadership in 1911, Lord Beaverbrook (then Max Aitken, a fellow Canadian, newspaper magnate and Conservative MP for Ashton-under-Lyne) nominated him for the leadership. The other nominations were Walter Long and Austen Chamberlain, more experienced men, but neither of whom were unanimously popular in the Party. Bonar Law was accepted as leader, causing Lloyd George to comment that 'the fools have stumbled on their best man by accident'.

Leading the opposition he constantly attacked Asquith and his administration, but when World War I broke out he put aside personal and party prejudices and offered Asquith the support of the Conservatives. In Asquith's coalition Government of 1915, he became Colonial Secretary during which time he closely witnessed Asquith's procrastination and Lloyd George's untiring energy, forcefulness and ability. He came to admire Lloyd George, whom he had once described as 'a tricky little Welsh jobber', and when Asquith resigned, Law knew without a doubt who should replace him. The King sent for Bonar Law to take over, but Law deferred to Lloyd George, offering to serve under him. Law was appointed Chancellor of the Exchequer and Leader of the House of Commons, as well as being a member of Lloyd George's War Cabinet.

Surrounded by their aristocratic colleagues, the fiery Welshman and the pessimistic Canadian complemented each other and made what Stanley Baldwin described as the most perfect partnership in political history. Lloyd George regarded the cautious Law as his greatest counsellor and submitted his ideas to him before putting them into practice. Law had a penchant for looking on the black side and if a plan or an argument could survive his immediate objections, Lloyd George knew he could proceed with it.

In 1917 a second tragedy struck Bonar Law, when his two eldest sons were killed in the war. Again the tragedy left him desolate, but again he was supported by his friends. When the war ended, Law and Lloyd George decided to go to the country again as a coalition and were returned with an enormous majority. Lloyd George remained prime minister and Law was appointed Lord Privy Seal and Leader of the House of Commons. For the next three years he worked under great pressure until his health began to fail, and in March 1921 he announced his retirement from public life. Playing no part in politics gave his health a chance to improve until, in 1922, when it looked as though Britain would go to war with Turkey for usurping Greek territory at Chanak, he wrote a letter to *The Times* stating that Britain needed a chance to recover herself and that she could not 'alone act as the policeman of the world'.

At this stage, the Conservatives decided to stand as a single party and Bonar Law, who had attended the meeting at the Carlton Club[27] where this was proposed, was in favour. Lloyd George consequently resigned and Bonar Law was invited by the King to form an administration. Law politely declined as he had not been re-elected leader of the Conservatives, but four days later, on 23 October 1922, after being re-elected at an ad hoc meeting of all Conservatives, he went to Buckingham Palace and kissed hands as Prime Minister.

His task of forming a Cabinet was not easy, as a number of Conservatives from the coalition government preferred to support Lloyd George. However, he succeeded, even if it was not, as Winston Churchill commented, from the first team. He appointed Lord Curzon as Foreign Secretary and Stanley Baldwin, a loyal supporter, as Chancellor of the Exchequer. Law drew up his Tranquillity Manifesto in which he appealed for 'tranquillity and freedom from adventures and commitments both at home and abroad' in an attempt to establish Britain's recovery after the exigencies of war. He then went to the country and despite the fact that the Conservatives were returned with a large majority, Bonar Law's life as premier was to prove second only to George Canning's in brevity, lasting for just 209 days. Although his health began to deteriorate rapidly his friends persuaded him not to resign. In April 1923, on his doctor's advice, he took a Mediterranean cruise, but was too weak to stay the course, and had to return home by train. He arrived on 19 May and offered his resignation the following morning. He died of inoperable throat cancer on 30 October 1923.

After the funeral service in Westminster Abbey, Asquith commented: 'It is fitting that we should have buried the unknown prime minister by the side of the Unknown Soldier'. Law may well indeed be the 'unknown prime minister', but this was because he chose to be unknown. Most of his work was done before he reached the highest office and, as Stanley Baldwin said, he gave his life for his country as much as if he had fallen in the war. But he did not give himself—his private life was his own.

Stanley Baldwin

Born 3 August 1867
Married Lucy Ridsdale (2 sons,
4 daughters)
Ministry 1923; 1924-9; 1935-7
(Conservative) – Kings George
V, Edward VIII
Died 13 December 1947. Buried
in Worcester Cathedral

Stanley Baldwin is the only premier to have held office during the reign of an uncrowned monarch—Edward VIII.

When Bonar Law resigned the premiership in May 1923 he was too ill to make the usual recommendation of a successor. So King George V, using his prerogative, consulted Lord Balfour, who had been a prime minister himself twenty years earlier. Balfour confirmed the King's own feeling, that in the prevailing post-war democratic atmosphere, the choice should be made from the House of Commons, not from the Lords. This precluded Lord Curzon, the Foreign Secretary, who considered himself the obvious successor, and the one who was chosen was Stanley Baldwin, the pipe-smoking, unobtrusive Chancellor of the Exchequer.

Baldwin, whom the offended Curzon described as 'a man of the utmost insignificance', was the son of Alfred Baldwin, Conservative MP for Bewdley, and a rich Midland industrialist, whose family had started iron works during the Industrial Revolution. Although his childhood was very happy, as an only child, with an invalid mother, Stanley was often very lonely and found his companionship in books. By an early age he had acquainted himself with most of the classics and all his life he never lost his love of literature. His reading, he once said, together with his experience in the family firm, proved of more educational value to him, than the unhappy days he had spent at Harrow and Trinity College, Cambridge.

When Baldwin left university, where he had gained a history degree, he intended to enter the Church. But he changed his mind and joined his father in one of the family businesses, eventually becoming financial director.Baldwin's chief aim in life was the brotherhood of man, and whilst he was in business he got to know every workman personally.

Like many successful businessmen of that time, Baldwin decided to try for Parliament and, when his father died in 1908, Baldwin took his place as MP for Bewdley. At the time the Liberals were in office, but when Lloyd George took over the wartime Coalition Government in 1916, Baldwin became Bonar Law's private secretary and then Financial Secretary to the Treasury. His rise was rapid, and by 1921 he was President of the Board of Trade, where he was responsible for the Safeguarding of Industries Act.

By now he was becoming increasingly distrustful of Lloyd George, whom he considered corrupting and devious and bent on destroying the political party system. Following the Conservatives' decision to stand as a single party after their disagreement with Lloyd George's foreign policy over the Turkey crisis, Baldwin made an eloquent speech at the subsequent Carlton Club meeting[27] in which he supported Bonar Law, inveighed against Lloyd George, and consequently helped to break the coalition Government.

In Bonar Law's ministry, which followed, he became Chancellor of the Exchequer. His first task was to arrange terms for settlement of the war debt with America. His inexperience as a cabinet minister led him to accept terms more stringent than had been hoped for, but he over-rode the political storm that followed.

A few weeks later, on 16 February 1923, he made his famous speech in the House in which he replied to a communist member who had outlined his party's intention when they governed the country. 'No gospel founded on hate will ever seize the hearts of the people of Great Britain,' he asseverated. 'The salvation for this country, and the whole of the world, is contained in four words: Faith, Hope, Love and Work.' This firmly entrenched Baldwin as a man of peace, love and honour, who cared for his country and its people, and when the ailing Bonar Law resigned Baldwin succeeded him, becoming prime minister on 22 May 1923.

He did not seek the premiership, and he did not particularly want it. When he was appointed Chancellor he had reached, he said, 'the limit of my ambitions', and looked forward to the day when he could go back to his home in Worcestershire 'to read the books I want to read, to live a decent life, and to keep pigs'. But this day was to be a long time coming. For Baldwin was to be prime minister three times.

His first ministry was shortlived, falling the following December when he went to the country seeking a mandate to reverse Bonar Law's free trade policy and to introduce tariffs to protect British industry. The Conservatives were returned without a sufficient majority and Ramsay MacDonald was asked to form the first ever Labour Government. Baldwin continued to lead the Conservative Party, which was now reunited, and when the Labour Government fell he became prime minister again, on 4 November 1924.

His main desire was peace—peace in industry, in the country, and in the world. He said:

> There is only one thing which I feel is worth giving one's whole strength to, and that is the binding together of all classes of our people in an effort to make life in this country better in every sense of the word. That is the main end and object of my life in politics.

At the end of a speech on the Trade Union Political Fund Bill, which proposed limiting the amount of support trade unions could give to the Labour Party, he prayed: 'Give peace in our time, O Lord'. His plea was answered and the bill rejected. Baldwin's moral courage inspired the people who loved and revered him, and his standing among them was unrivalled.

His ministry lasted until May 1929, and among its achievements were the Treaty of Locarno (a non-aggression pact between Britain, Belgium, France, Germany and Italy); a Pensions Act; a Franchise Act (extending votes to women over twenty-one); and the building of over one million houses. But his greatest achievement was his handling of the General Strike in 1926; by proclaiming a state of emergency, organising volunteers to maintain all essential services and refusing all further negotiations until the strike was called off, the TUC ended it on the ninth day. Baldwin was firm but had avoided provocation and was now at the peak of his popularity; as one newspaper wrote, he had, 'without ambitious intent, leapt into a position such as no prime minister had occupied since the days of William Pitt'. It is said that he could now have done anything, but in fact did nothing and failed to carry through a policy to pacify industry. Having confidence in his appointed ministers, he was content to leave them to their jobs; consequently his 'torpid, sleepy, barren government' as Lloyd George called it, lost the general election in May 1929. Again Baldwin was succeeded by Ramsay MacDonald, but he did not lose his popularity in the country.

The collapse of the Labour Government in the economic crisis of 1931 led to MacDonald's resignation and a National Government was formed in which MacDonald was reinstated as prime minister, and Baldwin became Lord President of the Council and deputy premier—though ostensibly subordinate to MacDonald, he was in fact the dominant figure. At the general election in November 1935, the National Government was returned, but MacDonald had lost some of his standing and Baldwin became prime minister for the third time.

The following year, 1936, was a crucial one for Baldwin. On 20 January, King George V died, and Baldwin was deprived of his constant support and friendship. Germany, repudiating the Treaty of Locarno, was rearming but Baldwin, although under attack from Winston Churchill for his inaction, still saw no need to do likewise. He left himself open to castigation in later years by telling the House in November, 1936, that although Hitler was rearming, Britain was in a pacifist mood and he did not believe that the country would give a mandate for rearmament.

Supposing I had gone to the country and said that Germany was rearming and that we must rearm, does anybody think that this pacific democracy would have rallied to that cry at that moment? I cannot think of anything that would have made the loss of the election from my point of view more certain.

Then came the Abdication crisis. King Edward VIII, a few months after his accession, announced his intention to marry Mrs Wallis Simpson, a twice-divorced American. At first the press restrained the news, but it eventually burst on a shocked nation on 2 December. On 11 December the King abdicated for himself and his heirs, and King George VI acceded. The children of Britain, unaware of the severity of the situation, ad libbed their Christmas carols: 'Hark the herald angels sing, old Ma Simpson's pinched our King.' It was due to Baldwin's handling of the crisis, in which he acted with delicacy and resolution as virtually sole intermediary between the King and his people, that the monarchy survived, unscathed, in those deeply troubled days. On 28 May 1937, shortly after the coronation of King George VI, he resigned. The King gave him the Garter, and created him Earl Baldwin of Bewdley. He retired to Astely Hall, his home in Worcestershire, to read his favourite books.

Baldwin was a serious Christian man. He was not a great orator, but endeared himself to the people through the medium of the wireless; with his beautiful, melodic voice he kept the public informed at all times. He had very few enemies, but his overwhelming popularity collapsed when he was blamed for the outbreak of World War II.

A cousin of Rudyard Kipling and a nephew of Burne Jones, the artist, Baldwin was a modest man who never overcame his surprise at becoming prime minister. 'The position of leader came to me when I was inexperienced, before I was really fitted for it, by a succession of curious chances that could not have been foreseen,' he told Asquith in 1926 after the fall of his first ministry. Then he formed his idea of what a prime minister ought to be, and that was as unlike Lloyd George as possible. He believed, above all, that a prime minister should be a chauvinist. Indeed, very early in his political career, when he was Financial Secretary to the Treasury, he wrote an anonymous letter to *The Times*, signed simple FST, appealing to the wealthy classes to tax themselves, according to their means, to help pay off the war debt and so help the less fortunate tax-payer. He had decided to purchase a war loan of £150,000—25% of his own estate, which he had estimated at £580,000—and return it to the country to help wipe off the debt. Few people responded to his appeal and it was years before the secret was revealed that FST stood for Financial Secretary to the Treasury and that the writer of the letter was in fact Baldwin. By this creed of love and generosity he lived until he died on 14 December 1947.

James Ramsay MacDonald

Born 12 October 1866
Married Margaret Gladstone
(3 sons, 3 daughters)
Ministry 1924–7; 1929–35
(Labour) – King George V
Died 9 November 1937. Buried
at Spynie, Lossiemouth

On 22 January 1924, James Ramsay MacDonald made history by becoming Britain's first Labour Prime Minister. After MacDonald had accepted the King's invitation to form an administration, George V wrote in his diary: '. . . I had an hour's talk with him, he impressed me very much, he wishes to do the right thing. Today 23 years ago dear grandmama died. I wonder what she would have thought of a Labour Government!' But if the King had misgivings about a Labour Government and what Queen Victoria would have thought, he was soon to lose them, for some weeks later he commented to Queen Alexandra, his mother; 'I must say they all seem to be very intelligent. They have different ideas to ours as they are all socialists, but they ought to be given a chance and ought to be treated fairly.'

Ramsay MacDonald was the illegitimate son of Anne Ramsay, a farm housekeeper, and John MacDonald, the head ploughman. He was born and brought up in the poor surroundings of his maternal grandmother's house in Lossiemouth. He was educated at the local board school at Drainie, where for 8d (4p) a month, his studies included Greek and Latin. He was an avid reader and had access to the dominie's books, as well as those in his grandmother's house, and copies of Dickens and Shakespeare which the local watchmaker lent him. When he was sixteen the dominie employed him as a pupil teacher and, two years later, he went to Bristol as assistant to a clergyman who ran a boys' club. Here he joined the Social Democratic Federation and so took his first step into political life, although he did not agree with

Marxist socialism perpetrated by the Federation. He then went to London, vowing that he would return to Lossiemouth a successful man, or not at all, but he was soon forced to return home following the breakdown of his health.

In 1888 MacDonald returned to London and became private secretary to Thomas Lough, the rich and popular Gladstonian Liberal candidate for Islington. He stayed with Lough for three years, during which time he made his acquaintance with the cultured middle classes. But MacDonald remained a socialist, joining most of the inchoate socialist organisations, including the Fabian Society, until he discovered the Independent Labour Party, formed in 1893, which represented the kind of socialism to which he aspired. At the general election of 1895 he unsuccessfully contested Southampton as an Independent Labour Party candidate. By now he was working as a journalist, contributing articles to newspapers, journals, and the *Dictionary of National Biography*.

In November 1896 MacDonald married Margaret Gladstone, the cultured, well educated daughter of a rich scientist and philanthropist, and niece of Lord Kelvin, the celebrated mathematician. Although their backgrounds were completely different they had much in common—not least of all their love of socialism. Through his wife MacDonald entered the middle class, and her money enabled him to travel. With her encouragement, he pressed ahead in the Labour movement, becoming a London county councillor, and, in 1900, secretary of the Labour Representation Committee (which became the Labour Party in 1906).

His political life became easier with his entry into the middle class, and his rise to power began. In 1906 he became Labour MP for Leicester, a seat he had contested and lost six years before because he was notoriously opposed to the Boer War. He spoke frequently in the House, and from the outset established a reputation for himself: 'a born parliamentarian' Lord Balfour called him. He and his wife continued to travel widely, visiting Europe, the United States, South Africa and India. In 1910 he published a book, *The Awakening of India*, which, apart from being considered the best book ever written about India by a tourist, helped to establish him as the most distinguished thinker, as well as spokesman, of the parliamentary Labour group of which in the following year, 1911, he became chairman.

Tragedy struck with the death of his wife on 8 September of

that year. Already the previous year, he had lost his mother and his youngest son and, without his wife's support and encouragement, MacDonald suffered a setback. His old aloofness and sensitivity returned, his social circle diminished, and he became a very lonely man.

During the industrial strife-torn years that followed he played a large part in putting the workers' case to Parliament, at the same time exhorting the workers to have patience. Meanwhile, the Labour Party was establishing itself, and MacDonald was criticised for being too moderate. On 5 August 1914, two days after war broke out, he resigned the chairmanship of the Parliamentary Labour Party because its members declined to support his proposal to oppose the government's demands for credits of £100 million to fight the war. He opposed the war and believed Britain was morally wrong to enter it. He was by now the most hated man in Britain. A campaign was waged against him in the press, in which he was accused of being pro-German, a traitor and a Bolshevik. One weekly magazine stooped so low as to publish a copy of his birth certificate, letting the world know that he was illegitimate. 'Thank God my mother is dead,' he told a friend, 'for this would surely have killed her.'

In the post-war election of 1918 he lost his seat at Leicester and was out of politics for the next four years until he was returned for the miners' stronghold of Aberavon in Wales. Despite his opposition to the war, he had retained the respect of his party and, on his return to Parliament, he became chairman and leader of the Labour Party and leader of the opposition, since Labour now outnumbered the Liberals. Consequently, when Stanley Baldwin succeeded Bonar Law, and failed to get a sufficient majority at his election in December 1923, Ramsay MacDonald was called to Buckingham Palace and asked by George V to form an administration.

And so, on 22 January 1924, MacDonald became prime minister of Britain's first ever Labour Government. But his ministry was shortlived. He held office as premier and as Foreign Secretary but this dual role put a strain on him, for he was over-conscientious and did not delegate. His concentration on foreign affairs led to his neglect of domestic issues and, since his Government could only exist on sufferance of the other two parties, it soon encountered difficulties.

MacDonald decided to call an election. Three days before

polling day the newspapers published the 'Zinoviev letter'.[31] Already, MacDonald, violently anti-Communist, had sent a note of protest to the Russian Embassy, but the public considered that the Government had been too soft with the Russians, and the result of the poll was an overwhelming defeat for the first Labour Government. Baldwin and the Conservatives ruled for the next five years until, in the election of 1929, Labour was returned and, with 287 seats, became for the first time the largest party in the House. MacDonald himself had stood for Seaham in Durham, and had achieved a record majority of 27,794. He was again asked to form an administration, but was still leading a minority government. MacDonald's government made history a second time, by the inclusion in the Cabinet of the first woman minister, Miss Margaret Bondfield, who became Minister of Labour and a Privy Councillor, and also with MacDonald travelling to America to become the first British prime minister to visit a president of the United States.

The Labour Government was again in difficulties at home. Unemployment, which stood at one million in 1929 when MacDonald took office, had reached 2.5 million by 1931, and the government could not afford to pay the unemployment benefit. A grave economic crisis ensued, with disruption in the Labour Party and loss of co-operation from the trade unions. MacDonald offered to resign, but was persuaded by the King that he was the man to lead the country through the crisis. MacDonald agreed to continue as prime minister provided he headed a National Government, to include the Conservative and Liberal leaders, Baldwin and Sir Herbert Samuel. Although he had lost the support of much of his own party, he continued as leader of the National Government (although Baldwin in fact held much of the power) which survived the next general election.

He had by now completely lost the support of the Labour Party and it was not long before the strains of office, personal loneliness and increasing blindness took their toll. He resigned on 7 June 1935, and was succeeded again by Baldwin. He then became Lord President of the Council. Although old and ill, he refused to give up, and at the general election in November he stood again for Seaham, but was defeated by the Labour candidate, Emanuel Shinwell. Nevertheless he persevered and at a by-election in January 1936 he was returned as MP for the Scottish universities. He died suddenly, on 9 November 1937, whilst on a sea voyage to South America.

MacDonald, founder of the Labour Party, was a peace-loving man, abhorring war, violence and Communism. He was a man of great charm, extremely cultivated, who overcame the stigma of illegitimacy, and educated himself to hold the highest position in the land. He understood people of all ranks and, throughout his life, maintained a fair and moderate stance.

Arthur Neville Chamberlain

Born 18 March 1869
Married Anne Vere Cole (1 son,
1 daughter)
Ministry 1937–40 (Tory) – King
George VI
Died 9 November 1940. Buried
in Westminster Abbey

Most prime ministers who were holding office when a war broke out did not survive in office, and Neville Chamberlain was no exception. Like Addington, Aberdeen and Asquith (*qqv*) before him, he had to be replaced by a tougher, warrior spirit.

Chamberlain, the youngest son of Joseph Chamberlain, the tariff reform champion, was educated at Rugby and Mason College, Birmingham, where he studied metallurgy and engineering design. When he was twenty-one he went to the Bahamas, to manage a 20,000 acre estate which his father had bought with the intention of growing sisal. For seven years he toiled in vain, the soil being too thin for the crop, and the venture had to be abandoned.

He returned to Birmingham, the city of his birth, where he became a prominent businessman, and very active in local affairs. He was elected a councillor in 1911 and Lord Mayor in 1915. Lloyd George, impressed by his ability and experience in local government, appointed him director general of the newly established Department of National Service in 1916. This was an unfortunate experience for Chamberlain, for Lloyd George instantly disliked him and, allowed him no authority nor the necessary equipment to tackle the task. Consequently he resigned after seven months and returned to Birmingham.

Meantime, in 1911, at the age of forty-two, Chamberlain had married Miss Anne Vere Cole, the twenty-eight year old daughter of an Indian Army officer. Despite the difference in their ages and backgrounds, they had much in common and she shared his love of music, books and, particularly, the countryside, for Chamberlain was a keen naturalist. Their marriage was idyllically happy, and she was a constant source of help and encouragement to him. Most of his achievements he attributed to her, saying gratefully, 'I could never have done it without Annie'.

Despite his setback with Lloyd George, he decided to stand for national politics, and in 1918 was returned as Conservative member for Ladywood. Although he supported the coalition Government, in which his brother Austen was Chancellor, he rejected suggestions that he should take government office, as he distrusted Lloyd George and refused to serve under him.

When the coalition fell in 1922 after the Carlton Club[27] meeting (at which Austen and Neville were, for the first time, in opposite camps), Neville became Postmaster General in Bonar Law's government, where he showed his sound judgement and administrative ability. His rise to power was rapid for, within a few months he became Minister of Health, and, in Baldwin's ministry, Chancellor of the Exchequer—from backbencher to second post in the Cabinet in just over a year, and all within five years of entering Parliament. But his stay at the Treasury was shortlived, for Baldwin was succeeded by Ramsay MacDonald's Labour Government. The Conservatives were returned within a few months, in October 1924, and Baldwin offered Chamberlain the Chancellorship, but Chamberlain successfully requested to become Minister of Health. Among his notable achievements were the Rating and Valuation Act (1925), and the Local Government Act (1929) which reformed the Poor Law and reorganised local government finance. From 1929–31 he was in opposition to MacDonald's Labour Government, but was made Chancellor of the Exchequer in his National Government, retaining the post under Baldwin. With unemployment standing at 2.5 million, and the Government unable to pay the unemployment benefit, an economic storm was raging, and in 1932 Chamberlain, with Cabinet approval, introduced the Import Duties Bill, which was passed later in the year. This was a special achievement for Chamberlain, since it was the culmination of all that his father, had fought for years' before, with his Protectionist campaign.

Chamberlain was now the obvious successor to Baldwin. He had no rivals and when Baldwin resigned on 28 May 1937, Neville Chamberlain, at the age of sixty-eight, became prime minister, achieving the position that his father and brother before him had narrowly missed. 'But I should never have made it if I hadn't had Annie to help me . . .' he told his sister. He was then elected leader of the Conservative Party.

War clouds were gathering in Europe, and already Spain was in the grip of civil war. Chamberlain declared that he would not be responsible for a war which he knew would destroy millions of people without doing his utmost to prevent it. Anthony Eden, the Foreign Secretary, resigned over Chamberlain's plans for dealing with Mussolini, and was replaced by Lord Halifax. Chamberlain then embarked upon his plan of appeasement with Hitler, which culminated in his visit, together with Mussolini and M Flandin, the French prime minister, to see Hitler in Munich, in September 1938. Here an agreement was reached that Britain and Germany would never go to war again. Chamberlain returned home a hero and was acclaimed as the man who had saved the world from war. To the crowds who clamoured round No. 10 Downing Street, he said, 'I believe it is peace for our time.' But his glory was shortlived for, by the following September, Hitler had broken his part of the bargain by greatly accelerating the rearmament of his forces and occupying Prague. When Germany attacked Poland, therefore, Chamberlain countered with Britain's declaration of war on her on 3 September 1939.

Chamberlain, his health deteriorating, was now a saddened old man who was under attack from all sides. With the failure of the British expedition to Norway in 1940 when that country fell to the Germans, the floodgates of abuse opened upon him. Lloyd George, his arch enemy, referring to Chamberlain's appeal for sacrifices, suggested that he should 'give an example of sacrifice, because there is nothing which can contribute more to victory than that he should sacrifice the seals of office'.

A motion of censure was moved against him, and in the

debate that followed the Government lost their huge majority. Chamberlain decided to form a National Government but, finding the Labour leaders would not serve under him, he resigned in favour of Winston Churchill on 10 May 1940. He remained in Churchill's coalition as Lord President of the Council, where his support proved invaluable, until, two months later, he had an operation for abdominal cancer, in September he had a relapse and resigned from the Cabinet. The King offered him the Garter and a peerage, both of which he declined preferring, he said, to die 'plain "Mr Chamberlain", like my father'. He died on 9 November 1940.

Chamberlain was a man of honour, and, as Churchill said after his death, he acted 'with perfect sincerity, and strove to the utmost of his capacity to save the world from the awful, devastating struggle' of World War II. Had it not been for the war, Chamberlain, the oldest entrant into politics to become prime minister, would no doubt have been one of the greatest.

Sir Winston Churchill

Born 30 November 1874
Married Clementine Hozier
(1 son, 4 daughters)
Ministry 1940–5; 1951–5
(Conservative) – King George
VI, Queen Elizabeth II
Died 24 January 1965. Buried
at Bladon, Oxfordshire

Winston Churchill was one of the greatest leaders Britain has ever known, yet had it not been for World War II he might well have slipped into history unsung. That war was his 'finest hour'.

Soldier, statesman, writer, painter, Nobel Prize-winner, this mighty genius sprang from a puny, premature baby, born unexpectedly at Blenheim Palace, where his parents were attending a ball. His father was Lord Randolph Churchill, third son of the 7th Duke of Marlborough, and a leading Tory poli-

113

tician. His mother was Jenny Jerome, the exquisitely beautiful daughter of the American Leonard Jerome, proprietor and editor of the *New York Times*.

From a preparatory school in Brighton, where he was described as the naughtiest small boy in the world, he went to Harrow, but he hated both school and learning, especially Latin. He could not comprehend the need to learn the vocative case of the first declension of Mensa, meaning O table, which he was told he would use when talking to a table. He was dismissed as impertinent and threatened with punishment, when he explained quite innocently that he did not talk to tables. After Harrow, where he achieved little academic merit, he succeeded, after sitting the entrance examination three times, in entering the Royal Military College, Sandhurst.

Churchill, the late-developer, now applied himself happily and seriously to his work with the result that his career at Sandhurst was brilliant; he passed out with honours, eighth in a class of 150 cadets, in December 1894, aged twenty. In March 1895 he was gazetted to the 4th Hussars. Meantime, at the beginning of the year, Lord Randolph Churchill died and Winston, who believed that his father thought him a fool, was grieved to be deprived of the chance to prove himself to his father. For the next three years he saw service in India and the Sudan, spending his off-duty time either in reading, writing, playing polo, or acting as war correspondent for the press. In 1899 he resigned his commission to take up politics. His first attempt, at a by-election in Oldham, failed. Then in October when the Boer War began, he sailed for South Africa as chief war correspondent for the *Morning Post*. With a four months' guaranteed contract of £250 a month, expenses paid, and complete freedom of reporting, he had acquired, at twenty-four, the best terms ever paid in British journalism. Shortly after his arrival in South Africa he was hitching a ride on an armoured train when it was ambushed. He was captured and taken to Pretoria as a prisoner of war. After three weeks he escaped over a lavatory wall and made his way to Durban, where he was proclaimed a hero. He had eluded the Boers, who had offered £25 for his return—dead or alive. Three years later, at a luncheon in London, he was introduced to General Louis Botha, leader of the Boer generals, who had come to England seeking financial help for their devastated country. Churchill proudly told Botha of his capture and escape;

the Boer leader then revealed that he had been Churchill's captor, and from this meeting sprang a firm friendship.

Returning to England the following year, 1900, Churchill tried again to enter Parliament. By virtue of his capture and escape his name was well known, and this helped him to succeed when he stood as Conservative candidate for Oldham at the election in October. Before taking his seat he carried out lecture tours of Britain and America, describing his South African adventure, for which he was paid £10,000.

In February 1901 he made his maiden speech, the first of many which were to show his frankness and originality of thought. In future years he was to be daubed a turncoat for changing parties, but Churchill was a free-thinker, not a one-party man, who was willing to work with any side which agreed with his principles and aims. Thus when the Tory Party split over Joseph Chamberlain's tariff-reform policy, Churchill took up the battle for free trade, believing it to be in the best interests of the poor and, on 31 May 1904, he crossed to the Liberals' side of the House and took his seat beside Lloyd George, becoming his ardent disciple.

When Campbell-Bannerman formed his ministry after the victorious Liberal landslide in December 1905, Churchill, now Liberal member for north-west Manchester, became Under-secretary of State for the Colonies. In Asquith's administration (1908) he became President of the Board of Trade, where he was responsible for setting up labour exchanges and unemployment insurance. Two years later, in 1910, he became Home Secretary and was responsible for the Mines Accidents Act (1910) and the Coal Mines Act (1911), which improved safety in the mines, provided pit-head baths, and prevented employment underground of boys under the age of fourteen; he was also concerned with penal reform. But perhaps his Home Secretaryship is best remembered by the siege of Sidney Street,[28] when he went down to the East End street to investigate the shoot-out between soldiers and criminals.

By now his courage and administrative ability were patently manifest to Mr Asquith, the prime minister, who, in October 1911, appointed him First Lord of the Admiralty. Here his zest for battle came to the fore: he spent the next three years reforming the Navy, and in July 1914 ordered a trial mobilisation of the whole fleet. Consequently, when war broke out on 4

August, the Navy was ready, and the British Expeditionary Force was carried to France unimpeded. Churchill's fame was running high, and for the next few months he played a successful and daring part in the strategy of the war. Then, in March 1915, came the failure of the Dardanelles Campaign,[29] for which Churchill was blamed. Although history has thrown a different light on the matter, he had at the time made so many enemies, particularly among the Tories who never forgave his apostasy, that he was used as the scapegoat. When the coalition Government was formed two months later, the price of Tory co-operation was Churchill's exclusion from the Cabinet and so he became Chancellor of the Duchy of Lancaster. This sinecure was too crippling for his active spirit, and in November he resigned and went to the front in France to command a battalion of the Royal Scots Fusiliers where, in the trenches at Ploegsteert, he learned the realities of war from practical experience.

He returned from France in the autumn of 1916. The following May, Lloyd George, who had now taken over the coalition from Asquith, appointed him Minister for Munitions, where his main achievement was to influence the development of the tank as an instrument of war. At the end of the war he transferred to the War Office and quickly organised the difficult task of demobilisation.

After the Russian Revolution (1917), Churchill made no secret of the fact that he wanted Britain to wage war against the Bolsheviks to end the 'foul baboonery of Bolshevism' as he called it. His efforts failed, but brought him into disfavour with those who sympathised with the revolting Russians.

In the election of 1922 Churchill lost his seat and was out of Parliament for two years until, in 1924, he was returned as Conservative member for Epping, having returned to that party when the Liberals put Labour in office. For the five years of Baldwin's second administration he was Chancellor of the Exchequer. These were stormy years for him, and he fell out of step with the people and his party leaders to such an extent, that he spent the following ten years, 1929–39, in the political wilderness. He used this miserable decade, when all political ears were closed to his warnings of the growing menace of Hitler's Germany, for writing, painting and reflecting. During the abdication crisis (see page 104) he tried, unsuccessfully, to form a 'King's Party' to return the King and himself to favour.

116

In 1939, when Chamberlain's appeasement policy with Hitler failed, as Churchill had repeatedly warned that it would fail, and war was declared on Germany on 3 September, Churchill was brought into office as First Lord of the Admiralty. His qualities of leadership and restless energy were immediately recognised and before long, the country demanded his appointment as its war leader. And so, on 10 May 1940 when Chamberlain resigned, King George VI sent for Churchill. 'I suppose you do not know why I have sent for you?' asked the King. 'Sir, I simply cannot imagine why,' replied Churchill, wryly. The King continued, 'I want to ask you to form a Government.' And so, at the age of sixty-five, the old war horse became head of one of the greatest ministries Britain has ever known. Like Lloyd George in World War I he formed a small War Cabinet, consisting of three Conservative members, with himself as prime minister, First Lord of the Treasury and Minister of Defence; Neville Chamberlain as Lord President of the Council; Anthony Eden as Foreign Secretary; and two Labour members, Clement Attlee as Lord Privy Seal and Arthur Greenwood as Minister Without Portfolio. He met the House of Commons on the 13 May and, asking for a vote of confidence, told them: 'I have nothing to offer but blood, toil, tears and sweat.' He went on to say that Britain's policy was 'to wage war by sea, land, and air, with all our might and with all our strength . . . against a monstrous tyranny, never surpassed in the dark lamentable catalogue of human crime.' And that our aim was 'Victory—victory at all costs . . .' That was the first of his many speeches which were not only to live forever, but were to be the spirit of Britain throughout the years of the war. With his indomitable courage, in words and deeds, he fused courage into the hearts of the forces and civilians alike, and led his country to victory. On 8 May 1945 he announced to the people of Britain that the war with Germany was ended, and again like Lloyd George, he led the House to St Margaret's, Westminster, to 'give humble and reverent thanks to Almighty God'.

His resignation from the coalition followed on 23 May and he became head of a caretaker Government until the general election on 5 July. Although he was immensely popular and hailed as the greatest war leader of all time, the electorate did not see him as the purveyor of the peace they wanted. The socialists were swept to victory with a resounding majority. Deeply offended by the country's rejection of him, Churchill spent the next five years as Conservative leader in opposition to Attlee's Government.

With the return to power of the Conservatives on 25 October 1951, Churchill became prime minister for the second time. One of his first tasks was to greet Elizabeth II, the new Queen, at the airport, on her return from her trip to East Africa, after King George VI had died suddenly on 6 February 1952. The following year the Queen gave him the Garter, which he had declined in 1945, and on 5 April 1955, at the age of 81, he resigned. However, he continued to represent Woodford, where he had first been returned as MP in 1945, and became 'father' of the House of Commons.

Soon after 8 o'clock on the morning of Sunday, 24 January 1965, Churchill died peacefully in his bed at his London home in Hyde Park Gate. Flags were lowered to half-mast, the State Bell at St Paul's tolled its parting knell and the lights of London were extinguished; Britain was plunged into a mourning unknown, save for the King himself. For three days his body lay in state at Westminster Hall, where thousands of people paid their last respects. After a state funeral, the music for which he had chosen himself, he was buried in the village churchyard at Bladon, in Oxfordshire, beside his parents and brother.

Churchill, who has been acclaimed as the greatest man of his time, was completely without fear; he never forgot his patrician birth, and refused to be overcome by adversity. Beneath his scowling face, and often grumpy, abrasive manner, he hid an irrepressible charm. He was a man of many talents, generous and magnanimous to a fault. Throughout his long eventful life he was sustained by two beautiful women, both of whom he adored: first his mother, whom as a child he saw as a fairy princess, and then his wife, whom he married in 1908. He was unique in many ways and is perhaps best understood through his many literary works.

Clement Richard Attlee (Earl Attlee)

Born 3 January 1883
Married Violet Millar
(1 son, 3 daughters)
Ministry 1945–51 (Labour) –
King George VI
Died 8 October 1967

Clement Attlee was a quiet unassuming man, who cherished a secret ambition to be a poet. He had no burning desire to be a national figure but rose rapidly to his position as premier by a succession of events rather than by the force of his personality.

He was born into a typical Victorian middle-class family. His father was a well-to-do City solicitor, his mother, a woman of independent means, was a social worker. Unlike most of his Labour Party contemporaries, there was nothing in Attlee's background and upbringing to force him into radical socialism—indeed, as a young man he was not particularly interested in politics.

After initial home tuition by his mother and a governess, Attlee went to Haileybury College and then to University College, Oxford, where he took a degree in history. He attended debates at the Oxford Union, but was too shy to speak at them. After graduating, he studied law at Lincoln's Inn and was called to the Bar in 1905. A few months later he went on a tour of London's dockland and visited a boys' club in Stepney, which was supported by Haileybury—and that visit was to be the turning point in his life.

He was immediately interested in helping the club and began by spending one night a week there. Two years later, in 1907, the club's manager resigned. Attlee took his place and moved into Stepney, where he lived for the next fourteen years. He was still painfully shy, but managed to overcome this enough to establish a rapport with the tough, working-class people of the East End. Their poverty, deprivation, unemployment and slum

119

conditions appalled him, and turned him to socialism. He joined the Independent Labour Party and became a propagandist, striving for social improvement. In 1910 he became secretary of Toynbee Hall, the Whitechapel educational and social settlement run by university graduates. He joined the Fabian Society, and lectured at the London School of Economics and elsewhere on Lloyd George's newly instituted insurance scheme.

During World War I he served as an officer in the South Lancashire Regiment, and fought at Gallipoli, where he was wounded, and in France. After the war he returned to his work in Stepney, where in 1919 he was elected Mayor. He held office for two years running and was an alderman for the next eight years.

In January 1922, at the age of forty, Attlee married Violet Millar. Their marriage, which produced four children, proved to be a long and happy one, and his wife was a constant source of encouragement to him. He moved from Stepney to Woodford Green, Essex, and in the autumn of that year he entered Parliament as member for Limehouse. And so began his steady, if unspectacular, rise to the top.

He voted for Ramsay MacDonald as leader of the Labour Party, became his parliamentary private secretary, and served in both his administrations when he became prime minister. When MacDonald formed a National Government in 1931, Attlee considered it 'the greatest betrayal in the political history of this country'. By now he was disillusioned with MacDonald and considered him vain and snobbish. Attlee then became deputy to George Lansbury, the new leader of the Parliamentary Labour Party, succeeding to the leadership himself when Lansbury resigned in October 1935. He continued as leader of the opposition until Chamberlain's resignation in 1940 when he joined Churchill's coalition as Lord Privy Seal. He had refused to serve under Chamberlain as head of the coalition. In 1942, Churchill appointed him deputy prime minister, and transferred him to Secretary of State for the Dominions. He was now officially in charge of domestic affairs while Churchill was engaged in activities abroad. In 1943 he became Lord President of the Council, still remaining deputy prime minister and a member of the War Cabinet. He made no spectacular impact during the war, but in his meticulous, dignified way he held his party and the coalition Government together.

When the war ended on 8 May 1945 Attlee was prepared to concede Churchill's wish to continue the coalition until the war with Japan had ended, but his Labour executive committee did not agree, and on 23 May Churchill dissolved the coalition and became head of a caretaker government until the election on 5 July. Labour was swept into power with a majority which shocked even Attlee. And at the age of sixty-two, Clement Attlee became prime minister of Britain's first ever Labour majority Government.

Within forty-eight hours of kissing hands with King George VI as prime minister Attlee formed his strong, efficient administration, which included Ernest Bevin as Foreign Secretary, Aneurin Bevan as Minister of Health, Sir Stafford Cripps as President of the Board of Trade, and Attlee himself as Minister of Defence.

Attlee was by now a very experienced politician and, in its six years, his administration accomplished an astounding record of social and economic reform. Among its achievements were the introduction of the National Health Service; the nationalisation of the coal, electricity, gas, railway and steel industries, a huge building and rebuilding programme which included the establishment of new towns, and a new national insurance scheme. In foreign affairs, he coped with the dismantling of the British Empire (granting independence to India), the airlift during the Russian blockade of Berlin (1948–9) and the formation of the North Atlantic Treaty Organisation to prevent the infiltration of Russia into Western Europe. One bright spot in those troublesome postwar years was the wedding on 20 November 1947, of Princess Elizabeth to Prince Philip, when the country rejoiced in British pomp and ceremony.

Labour was returned at the general election in 1950, but with a considerably reduced majority. After eighteen months of struggling on Attlee decided to go to the country. Both Ernest Bevin and Stafford Cripps had died, and internal strife was splitting the party. Aneurin Bevan resigned and persuaded Harold Wilson to do likewise. Attlee himself fell ill with duodenal ulcers. At the election in October 1951 the Conservatives were returned with a majority of sixteen. Labour had lost nineteen seats, despite the fact that they polled nearly fourteen million votes—the largest number ever gained by one party in political history. Attlee, who since 1950 had represented West Walthamstow as

Limehouse had disappeared in a boundary redistribution, was returned with a slightly reduced majority. He immediately tendered his resignation and Winston Churchill became prime minister for the second time and a few days later the King awarded Attlee the Order of Merit.

He led the opposition for the next four years and, on 6 December 1955, after Anthony Eden had become prime minister of the Conservative government, he retired from the party he had led for twenty years. The following day the Queen made him an earl, and in April 1956 he received the Garter.

He spent his retirement taking part in debates in the Lords, travelling on lecture tours at home and abroad, and writing; in 1954 he published a volume of memoirs *As It Happened*. He died of pneumonia on 8 October 1967.

Attlee, who was much underestimated, may not go down to posterity as one of Britain's greatest prime ministers, but he was a very good administrator, capable of choosing and leading a very efficient team. A mild-mannered man, he spoke only when it was necessary, but then soundly and wisely. From those early days in Stepney, when he realised that the basis of society was wrong, he dedicated himself to socialism to fight the inequality of man.

Sir Anthony Eden (Earl of Avon)

Born 12 June 1897
Married (1) Beatrice Beckett (2 sons); (2) Clarissa Churchill (no children)
Ministry 1955–6 (Conservative) – Queen Elizabeth II
Died 14 January 1977. Buried at Alvediston, Wiltshire

When Winston Churchill retired in April 1955, he was succeeded by the man he considered to be his political heir—Anthony Eden. Not since the days of Salisbury and Balfour, half a century before, had a politician been so groomed for the job. But for Eden, who had proved himself a brilliant foreign secretary, his premiership was a complete fiasco, and was brought to an end after two years by the political storm caused through his handling of the Suez crisis.

The third son of Sir William Eden, a rich, eccentric Durham baronet, he was educated at Eton and Christ Church, Oxford, where he took a degree in Oriental languages. In World War I, before going to Oxford, he served in France as an officer in the King's Royal Rifle Corps, winning the MC for rescuing his severely wounded platoon sergeant.

After Oxford, in the election of December 1923 he was returned as Conservative member for Warwick and Leamington.

The month before the election, on 5 November, he married Beatrice Beckett at St Margaret's, Westminster. This marriage, which produced two sons, the eldest of whom was killed in World War II, ended in divorce in 1950. Two years later, at the age of fifty-five, he married Clarissa Churchill, the beautiful thirty-two year old niece of Sir Winston.

When Eden entered Parliament Ramsay MacDonald's first Labour Government was in power. His early speeches revealed his concern for an increased air force and his interest in foreign affairs. He soon came under the fatherly eye of Stanley Baldwin, and in 1925 became Parliamentary Private Secretary at the Home Office in Baldwin's second administration. The following year he held the same position to Austen Chamberlain at the Foreign Office, until Ramsay MacDonald once again succeeded Baldwin in 1929. For the next two years he was out of office, then in MacDonald's national government of 1931 he became Under-secretary at the Foreign Office. Eden was on the way up. Extremely handsome, immaculately dressed, with an attractive voice and charming manners, he was the golden boy of the Tory party, and at the election in October 1931 he won a resounding victory, gaining one of the largest majorities in the country—29,000 votes more than his Labour opponent. He was now mainly concerned with the League of Nations[30] and became a familiar figure at Geneva.

In Baldwin's third administration of 1935 he became Minister for League of Nations Affairs, and soon established himself as a brilliant negotiator, and upholder of the League's principles. Towards the end of the year, when Sir Samuel Hoare, the Foreign Secretary, was forced to resign over his handling of the Abyssinian crisis, Eden became his successor—at thirty-eight the youngest Foreign Secretary since Lord Grenville took office at the age of thirty-two a century and a half before.

His two years of office were fraught with the threats of Hitler's and Mussolini's aggressive policies in Europe, which he tried to solve through negotiations with Hitler. Then, when Chamberlain took office after Baldwin's resignation, Eden, disagreeing with Chamberlain's appeasement policy and interference in foreign office affairs, resigned on 20 February 1938. Speaking in the House of Commons of his resignation he said:

Of late the conviction has steadily grown upon me that there has been too keen a desire on our part to make terms with others rather than that they should make terms with us. This never was the attitude of this country in the past. It should not, in the interests of peace, be our attitude today.

With the outbreak of World War II in September 1939, Eden re-entered the Chamberlain government as Dominions Secretary, and in Churchill's coalition became Secretary of State for War (1940), where he was responsible for setting up the Home Guard. The following December Churchill transferred him to the Foreign Office, where his performance was brilliant. From 1942 he was both Leader of the House of Commons and Foreign Secretary, and during this time Churchill had informed King George VI that if he (Churchill) became a war casualty, he recommended Anthony Eden, 'who is in my mind the outstanding minister in the largest political pary in the House of Commons' as his successor.

After the war, from 1945–51 Eden became deputy leader of the opposition to Attlee's Labour Government, returning as Foreign Secretary in Churchill's administration of 1951. Again he faced troubled years. The Cold War between Russia and the West was at its peak and there was trouble in Persia and Egypt. Despite failing health—he was seriously ill in 1953 and underwent three operations—his expertise as a negotiator settled the critical issues and in 1954 he received the Garter for his services.

When Churchill retired in April 1955, Eden received the seals of office. But for Eden it was a fateful day. The man who had been revered as one of the world's finest foreign secretaries, was no prime minister. He became vain, sensitive, and jealous of his colleagues, interfering in the organisation of their departments, particularly the Foreign Office, which he still wished to control. This was the very thing he complained of when he was Foreign Secretary under Chamberlain. His downfall began soon after Egypt's General Nasser nationalised the Suez Canal (of which Britain was a principal shareholder) in July 1956, causing a war between Israel and Egypt. Eden, acting completely out of character (no doubt through ill-health) and believing he could prevent the war from spreading, sanctioned the bombing of Egyptian forces and the sending in of airborne troops to Port Said to fight the Egyptians. Shortly after, an armistice was agreed and the United Nations intervened. Meantime, a political storm raged in the House of Commons and there was consternation in the country. Unable to stand the strain caused by these events, Eden fell seriously ill and his doctors advised that he could not carry on the strenuous task of the premiership. On 9 January 1957 he handed his resignation to the Queen. Two days later he resigned from his constituency.

He spent the remaining years of his life in political seclusion, his health declining steadily. In 1961 he was created Earl of Avon. The perfect Englishman, he had always made it clear that he wanted to die in England, and his wish was granted. In January 1977, he was taken seriously ill whilst on holiday in Florida, and James Callaghan, the prime minister, ordered an RAF plane to bring him home. He died peacefully, five days later, in his own home at Alvediston, Wiltshire.

Harold Macmillan

Born 10 February 1894
Married Lady Dorothy
Cavendish (1 son, 2 daughters)
Ministry 1957–63 (Conserva-
tive) – Queen Elizabeth II

Harold Macmillan succeeded Anthony Eden as prime minister on 10 January 1957 following a period of economic growth and prosperity, but his seven years in office were to see changes both at home and in the Commonwealth—changes which were to be the downfall of the man who enjoyed great popularity during the early years of his premiership.

Like Sir Winston Churchill, Macmillan is half American. His mother was Helen Belles, a doctor's daughter from Indiana, his father was Maurice Crawford Macmillan, son of Daniel Macmillan, a poor Scottish crofter, who founded the famous publishing house of Macmillan & Co, and raised his family to the upper middle class.

Harold, the youngest of three sons, spent a happy childhood in a loving family. At the age of twelve he went to Eton, but had to leave prematurely because of illness. He then had various private tutors, among whom was Ronald Knox, the Catholic author, who had a 'profound influence' upon him. In 1912 he won an exhibition to Balliol College, Oxford, where he gained a first class degree in classics.

He served with the Grenadier Guards during World War I and was twice wounded, first at the battle of Loos (1915) and later at the battle of the Somme (1916), when his pelvis was shattered by machine-gun bullets. This second wound, which did not heal properly until 1920, kept him in hospital for two years. In 1919 he went to Ottawa as ADC to the Duke of Devonshire, the Governor General of Canada, and fell in love with the Duke's nineteen year old daughter, Lady Dorothy Cavendish. They returned to England the following year and were married at St Margaret's, Westminster, on 21 April 1920.

Their marriage was idyllic, and Lady Dorothy, through her 'wise advice and loyal support' helped him to sustain both the burdens and the excitements of life. After their marriage, Macmillan joined the family publishing firm, but soon a career in politics began to interest him. Lady Dorothy came from a long line of politicians who had ruled the Whig aristocracy in the eighteenth century, and through her Macmillan was introduced into both high politics and high society.

His first attempt to enter Parliament at Stockton in 1923 failed, but the following year, when Ramsay MacDonald's government fell following the publication of the Zinoviev letter,[29] he was returned for Stockton with a huge majority. Stockton was a working-class district and the deprivation and poverty that he saw there in those early days was to evoke a comment years later when, as Prime Minister, he compared the more prosperous days of his ministry with the squalid conditions of that time that were 'not fit for heroes to live in'.

In July 1957, when there was full employment and high wages, and the working-classes became part of an affluent society which could afford to buy the material comforts of modern life, Macmillan, remembering those far-off days, addressed an audience in Bedford:

Let us be frank about it, most of our people have never had it so good . . . Go round the country . . . and you will see a state of prosperity such as we have never had in my lifetime —nor indeed ever in the history of this country.

Although Macmillan made this speech as an expression of his sincere delight at the social improvement of working people, those five words 'never had it so good', were to be taken out of context and used for and against him as the media thought fit. Even the Archbishop of Canterbury, Geoffrey Fisher, referred to Macmillan's 'materialism'. But no amount of explanation on Macmillan's part could assuage the criticism—his intent had been misconstrued and public opinion was not to be changed.

Macmillan's early political career was undistinguished. He entered the House as a supporter of Stanley Baldwin, then heading his second administration, but soon joined a group of left-wing Young Conservatives, nicknamed the YMCA, who were intent on social reform and economic planning. He wrote a series of books and pamphlets during the years 1929–39 which revealed his social conscience and moderate thinking. Although he was an able politician he was regarded as a rebel for his unorthodox views and was not offered a place in any government until Churchill, whose supporter he had since become, appointed him Parliamentary Secretary to the Ministry of Supply in his coalition government of 1940. In February 1942 he moved to the Colonial Office as Parliamentary Under-secretary.

Both these posts were minor ones, and Macmillan, now forty-eight and despairing of ever making his mark in parliament, was thinking of giving it all up and going back to publishing. Then Churchill appointed him Minister Resident at the Allied Headquarters in North-West Africa, which the Allies had just invaded. He was now a Cabinet minister—'in the big stuff' as he called it—and he handled this important post with skilful diplomacy.

On returning to England in May 1945 Macmillan became Secretary for Air in Churchill's caretaker Government, but, in the post-war election two months later, which was won by Labour, he was overwhelmingly defeated at Stockton-on-Tees. However, a safe seat was found for him at Bromley, Kent, and in a by-election in November he was returned, and he retained the seat until his retirement from politics in 1964.

Apart from his brief spell in Churchill's caretaker Government, Macmillan had been away from Westminster for three years, and on taking his seat in opposition to Attlee's Government he found, as Asquith had found twenty-five years earlier after the events of World War I, a completely changed House. He felt, he said, like Rip Van Winkle—and the new-style Labour members, who considered his patronising Edwardian air an anachronism, regarded him as such. After his high-powered job in the Mediterranean Macmillan did not enjoy his work in opposition.

When the Conservatives were returned to power in 1951 he hoped again for a top job. But, to his disappointment, Churchill offered him the Ministry of Housing. Reluctantly he accepted the post, and it turned out to be the happiest three years of his life. In that time he instigated the building of nearly one million houses and established a reputation for getting things done. In October 1954 he became Minister of Defence, and six months later, in April 1955, when Eden had become prime minister, he was appointed Foreign Secretary. He was at the Foreign Office for just eight months, but during that time the Austrian Peace Treaty was signed in May, the 'Big Four' met at the first Summit Meeting in Geneva in July, and the diplomats Burgess and Maclean defected to Russia in November. On 20 December Macmillan took over from 'Rab' Butler as Chancellor of the Exchequer and introduced premium bonds, in his one budget the following April.

Anthony Eden resigned through ill-health and the next day, using the Royal prerogative as King George V had done in choosing Baldwin, the Queen summoned Macmillan to Buckingham Palace and asked him to form a ministry. He accepted, but pessimistically informed the Queen that it could not last for more than six weeks. The country was incensed over the Suez crisis,[32] and in any case the press had confidently tipped 'Rab' Butler as Eden's successor. But the Queen had consulted Lords Salisbury and Kilmuir, who in turn had consulted the Cabinet members and backbenchers, and the overwhelming consensus of opinion was in favour of Macmillan.

He formed his ministry which he and most others expected to be a stop-gap administration. Before long he had restored the country's confidence in the Government, established good relations abroad and helped to effect a thaw in the Cold War with Russia. As Baldwin used the wireless to take himself into the homes of the people, so Macmillan used television, where he could be seen as well as heard. His affable, fatherly manner, pleasing voice, and obvious concern, made him a great favourite. There was an economic boom when Britain 'had never had it so good'. Riding on the crest of this wave, he went to the country for a vote of confidence in the Government, and the Conservatives were retured with an increased majority.

Macmillan then went on a tour of Africa, where he used the second of his famous phrases—'the wind of change'. Sensing agitation in the Commonwealth, Macmillan told the South African Parliament that 'The wind of change was blowing throughout the continent.' But not only did the wind of change blow in the Commonwealth, it was soon to blow in Britain. And 'Supermac', 'Macwonder', the affluent society's big daddy, was

129

to become the victim of circumstances. The earlier phase of the domestic economic boom was now followed by slow growth and inflation; moreover, his efforts to join the Common Market were thwarted by France's General de Gaulle in 1963. Britain was hit by a financial crisis, unemployment rose to almost one million and consequently the Government was losing many of its seats in by-elections. In a drastic effort to save the situation, Macmillan carried out an unprecedented purge of the Cabinet in which he sacked six ministers.

Then the final axe fell. Vassall, the Foreign Office spy, was sent to prison, together with two Fleet Street journalists who would not reveal their sources of information regarding the case. The 'Profumo Affair' then exploded, with the resignation of John Profumo, the War Minister, over a call-girl scandal.

By now Harold Wilson, a master in opposition, was leading the Labour Party. With his savage attacks, and Fleet Street taking their revenge for the imprisoned journalists, Macmillan and his Government suffered. But with his usual calmness, Macmillan rode the storm, despite taunts that he was now too old at the age of seventy to lead the party and the country. Despite his television appearances in which he expressed his hope of leading the Conservative Party through another election, he was forced to resign through ill-health shortly after entering hospital for an operation. His intention to resign was read to the Conservative Party Conference at Blackpool in October 1963. On 19 October he sent his resignation to the Queen and was succeeded by Sir Alec Douglas-Home. Macmillan then rejoined his publishing firm, and began writing his memoirs.

Sir Alec Douglas-Home

Born 2 July 1903
Married Elizabeth Alington
(1 son, 3 daughters)
Ministry 1963–4 (Conservative)
– Queen Elizabeth II

Sir Alec Douglas-Home, formerly Earl Home, was the first member of the House of Lords to take the premiership since Lord Salisbury in 1895.

Born Alexander Frederick Douglas-Home, he was the eldest son of Lord Dunglass, 13th Earl of Home. Educated at Eton and Christ Church, Oxford, he was not particularly interested in politics, but when Lloyd George commented that the new democratic age needed young men with new ideas, he decided to do his duty towards his country. He entered Parliament in 1931 as Conservative member for South Lanark and became a supporter of MacDonald's National Government.

In 1937 he became parliamentary private secretary to Neville Chamberlain then, finding himself out of office following Chamberlain's resignation in 1940, he applied to join the Lanark-shire Yeomanry for active service. A medical examination revealed a tubercular condition of the spine (caused by his falling against a tree stump and bruising his back some years earlier) and, after an operation, he spent two years flat on his back, encased in a plaster-cast. He spent his months of enforced inactivity reading and studying the origins and workings of Soviet Communism, and this knowledge proved extremely useful when he was Foreign Secretary years later. In 1944 he returned to Westminster, but lost his seat in the 1945 election and was out of politics for five years until, in 1950, he was returned again for Lanark. In July 1951 his father died and he was elevated to the House of Lords as the 14th Earl of Home.

Shortly afterwards Churchill appointed him Secretary of State at the Scottish Office. When Eden became prime minister in 1955 he transferred him to the post of Secretary of State for Commonwealth Relations. Two years later, when Macmillan took office he added to this post Lord President of the Council and Leader of the House of Lords, and in July 1960, he was appointed Foreign Secretary—a position in which Home was able to demonstrate his true abilities.

The Foreign Office had not been occupied by a member of the House of Lords since Lord Halifax's appointment just before World War II, and Home's appointment received some criticism. Hugh Gaitskell, then Leader of the opposition, pronounced it 'constitutionally objectionable' and moved a censure motion. The motion was rejected when Macmillan stated that he should not be deprived of the 'best man for the job' because of an accident of birth. Labour opposition did not forget Home's 'accident of birth' and used it against him in later years.

During his three years at the Foreign Office, Lord Home endeared himself to the people. He was honest, outspoken and unafraid. He was not prejudiced by personal ambition or the fear of losing his seat, which was one advantage of his being in the Lords. It was not surprising, therefore, that he was recommended to succeed Macmillan.

When Home became Prime Minister, on 19 October 1963, the Conservative Party was not very popular in the House or in the country; they had been in office for twelve years and it was generally considered that a change of government was needed. The Vassall and Profumo scandals had not been forgotten, nor had France's rejection of Britain's application to join the Common Market (see page 138); add to this a peer of the realm taking the premiership and the plebeian Mr Wilson, as leader of the opposition, had all the ammunition he needed for his attack. Wilson lashed out immediately after the announcement of Lord Home's appointment: what could that 'elegant anachronism' from 'his sheltered aristocratic background' know of the problems of ordinary families . . . and how indeed could 'a scion of an effete establishment' comprehend, let alone lead, the new scientific revolution? Wilson continued: 'After half a century of democratic advance, of social revolution, the whole process has ground to a halt with a 14th earl.'

Appearing on television a few days later, Lord Home, asked if he did know how the other half lived, replied that he did not believe there were two halves to the nation. He pointed out that when he was in Parliament he represented, and lived among, a mining constituency for twenty years, and that as he was a farmer he knew about farms; so of course he knew how other people lived. As far as being the 14th earl was concerned, he quipped, he presumed Mr Wilson was the 14th Mr Wilson.

Lord Home survived this initial attack, but he felt that in the new age of the up and coming young executive, being a peer might be a disadvantage. So on 23 October he disclaimed his peerage for life, and became known as Sir Alec Douglas-Home. Parliament, which was due to meet the next day, was prorogued while a seat was found for him in the Commons. On 6 November he was returned for the safe Conservative seat of Kinross and West Perthshire. He was then formally elected leader of the

Party and took his seat in the Commons when the House met on 12 November. He did not have an easy task in forming his Cabinet. Both Enoch Powell and Iain Macleod refused to serve under him. However, 'Rab' Butler agreed to take the Foreign Office and he had the support of able young men such as Edward Heath and Reginald Maudling.

His ministry lasted for just one year, but he was not crushed by the savage attacks of Mr Wilson, as had been predicted. He brought the Conservative Party back to order after it had fallen into disarray following Macmillan's Cabinet purge, and prepared the way for the next general election, which he knew was imminent. When it came on 15 October 1964, Home and Wilson campaigned vigorously, Labour gaining the victory, with 317 seats against the Conservatives' 303, and Liberals' 9. On 17 October Sir Alec conceded defeat and handed his resignation to the Queen. He then became leader of the opposition until he graciously relinquished the leadership of the Conservative Party in favour of Edward Heath in 1965. When Heath became prime minister in 1970, Sir Alec was appointed Foreign Secretary, which post he held until the fall of the Conservative Government in 1974.

Sir Alec, perhaps the last of the aristocratic and Eton–educated Tory prime ministers, took office too late in his life, when a new era had already dawned. He did not seek high office, but accepted it as his duty when it was thrust upon him. He was rich, intelligent, and born to a heritage which gave him the confidence to cope with high office. He also had strong religious convictions, accepting Christianity as part of his everyday life, and was not afraid to incorporate his moral and religious beliefs into his speeches, which endeared him to believers and dissidents alike.

Sir Harold Wilson

Born 11 March 1916
Married Mary Baldwin (2 sons)
Ministry 1964–70; 1974–6
(Labour) – Queen Elizabeth II

When Harold Wilson took office in October 1964 he was only the third Labour prime minister to be appointed since Ramsay MacDonald brought the Labour Party to power in 1924.

Wilson, the son of a north-country industrial chemist, was educated at Wirral Grammar School and Jesus College, Oxford, where he gained a first-class degree in Philosophy, Politics and Economics. After graduating, he lectured in Economics at New College and the following year, 1938, became a Fellow of University College, and research assistant to the Warden, Sir William Beveridge.

When war broke out in 1939 he volunteered for the Army, but was drafted into the Civil Service and by 1943 had become Director of Economics and Statistics at the Ministry of Fuel and Power. His experience in this post led him to write his first book, *A New Deal for Coal*, which was published in 1947, and he was awarded the OBE for his wartime services.

After the war he left the Civil Service to return to Oxford as a lecturer in economics. This same year, 1945, he decided to enter politics and was returned with a majority of more than 7,000 as Labour member for Ormskirk, Lancashire, in the general election which brought Labour back to power. When Attlee formed his administration he made Wilson Parliamentary secretary to the Ministry of Works. And so began Wilson's climb to the top. He was twenty-nine, the youngest member of the ministerial team and one of the youngest members in the Commons. For an ambitious young man his start was a good one, for he never sat on the back benches. Applying himself diligently to the task he soon mastered parliamentary procedure and the art of speaking in the House. In March 1947 he became Secretary for Overseas Trade, and six months later was promoted to the Cabinet as President of the Board of Trade—the youngest Cabinet minister for more than a century.

When he took over the Board of Trade, the country was still in the grip of rationing and suffering from the austerity of his predecessor, Stafford Cripps. So the people hoped that the young forward-looking Wilson would relieve some of their difficulties. But Wilson did not lift controls; instead, he spoke in the House about setting aside thoughts of luxury and easy living . . . of rebuilding the war-shattered economy and laying the foundations for a higher standard of living and industrial greatness for the nation. But the war-weary and deprived British were not impressed by his easy rhetoric.

Although he was constantly accused of mismanaging the Board of Trade he remained there during Attlee's second term of office after the election of 1950, in which he was returned for Huyton, as Ormskirk was affected by a boundary redistribution and was lost to the Conservatives. Wilson had by now become a follower of Aneurin Bevan—'Nye's little dog', he was called— and when Aneurin Bevan resigned from the government in April 1951, Wilson resigned too.

In the election of 1951 the Conservatives were returned to power and remained there for the next thirteen years. During this time Wilson was acting as economic adviser to a timber exporting company, then in 1963, following Hugh Gaitskell's death, Wilson became leader of the Labour Party. He was a brilliant leader, and united the quarrelsome Labour Party and held it together successfully for twenty-three years, until his resignation in 1976. He believes that party unity is the key to success.

As leader of the opposition he campaigned against Sir Alec Douglas-Home in the election of October 1964, slating Home for his earldom and protesting vehemently that 'a scion of an effete establishment' should be elected to lead the new scientific revolution. Wilson campaigned with a determination to win, and he brought the Labour Party to a very narrow victory. His term of office was not an easy one. His left-wing ministers and the unions were troublesome, and wildcat strikes were causing disruption throughout industry. But Wilson, as always, rode the storm, and above all maintained a united party.

Wilson was a politician to be reckoned with—one Tory MP described him as the best parliamentarian of our age; others have called him the Houdini of politics. Certainly he could get himself out of any mess he got himself into. Wilson was a tactician—meticulous and persistent. He has an incredible memory, great tenacity, and above all, he always did his homework and was ready for anybody and any situation.

In March 1966 Wilson went to the country and Labour was again returned to power. But in the election of 1970, despite the sweeping victory predicted by the opinion polls, they lost to the Conservatives and Wilson was replaced by Edward Heath. Heath took the country into the Common Market and Wilson promised to get it out again. Heath then had a confrontation with the unions over his industrial policy. This caused him to go to the country, and the ensuing election in February 1974 was fought on a Unions and Common Market issue. Labour won. But Labour had by now decided to negotiate terms for a better deal for Britain in the Common Market, and in June 1975 the country, for the first time in history, took part in a referendum, in which the majority of British people voted in favour of remaining in the European Economic Community.

Meantime, in October 1974, the Labour Party had been returned again and Harold Wilson was prime minister for the fourth time—the only politician to achieve this since Gladstone. There was much speculation that Wilson was determined to emulate Gladstone as the Grand Old Man of politics, but, for his own reasons, he suddenly announced to a surprised nation on 16 March 1976 that, when a new leader was found, he would resign from the leadership of the party and so from the premiership.

After a three-week battle for the title, James Callaghan emerged as leader. Wilson handed his resignation to the Queen on 5 April 1976, and for the first time in his thirty-one years in parliament, sat on the back benches. Eighteen days later, on St George's Day, the Queen conferred on him a Knighthood of the Garter.

His resignation honours list caused much speculation in the press as to who was responsible for the selection. Among those honoured was Marcia Williams, Wilson's private and personal secretary, who was elevated to the peerage as Lady Falkender. The following year, Joe Haines, Wilson's political press secretary, published a book in which he suggested that Marcia Williams had been responsible for the list, and that during Wilson's premiership she had had access to his cabinet papers. In the press, accusations and denials came from all sides, until eventually they died a natural death, leaving history to reveal the truth.

Although Wilson appeared to be a hard-hitting politician, he was a very sensitive man, often inwardly unsure of himself, and his cutting invective in the House was his way of silencing his critics. His wife, Mary, is a shy, retiring woman, who preferred to remain in the background reading and writing poetry. She did not believe in pushing a man—'if he has it in him he will make it on his own,' she believed. Harold Wilson certainly did make it, and a good account of his achievement is written in his book *Personal Record*.

Edward Heath

Born 9 July 1916
Unmarried
Ministry 1970–4 (Conservative)
– Queen Elizabeth II

When Edward Heath became prime minister in June 1970, he confounded all opinion polls and newspaper speculation, who had predicted a resounding victory for Labour. But the people were tired of the Unions 'running the country' under Labour and were prepared to give the Tories, with their new-look leader a chance. Heath was the first non-public school Tory prime minister since Bonar Law, almost half a century earlier, and in the age of the young executive, it was hoped that he would bring a new image to the Tory Party.

The son of William Heath, a builder from Broadstairs in Kent, he was educated at Chatham House Grammar School at Ramsgate, and Balliol College, Oxford, which he claimed 'opened all doors for me'. He became president of both the Oxford Union and the University Conservative Association, and formed the Balliol Choir. During the war he served in Europe as an officer in the Royal Artillery. When he left the army, he decided to enter politics. After some initial disappointments he was adopted as Conservative candidate for Bexley, Kent, in 1947 and was returned with a small majority in the election of 1950. Meantime, to support himself, he had been editor of the *Church Times*, and a trainee in a merchant bank.

When he entered the House of Commons Attlee was Labour prime minister, and Heath joined the 'One Nation' group which favoured European unity, this being the subject of his very successful maiden speech. In 1951 he became an assistant whip, and in 1955 Chief Whip, and as such held the shattered Tory party together after the Suez crisis[32] and the collapse of the Eden Government. Heath then became a supporter of Macmillan and in 1960 was appointed Minister of Labour. The following year he became Lord Privy Seal and Macmillan's 'Mr Europe', travelling thousands of miles in pursuit of Britain's entry into the European Economic Community (Common Market). Despite his own conviction he could not overcome General de Gaulle's constant objections to Britain's entry to the EEC, but his persistence demonstrated that he was a dedicated politician and common marketeer.

Heath became a supporter of Sir Alec Douglas-Home, the new premier, following Macmillan's resignation in 1963, and was appointed President of the Board of Trade. He had little time to show his ability, for Home's administration was shortlived and was replaced by Harold Wilson's Labour Government in October 1964.

For the next six years Heath was out of office, but during this time, in July 1965, he had replaced Sir Alec Douglas-Home as Conservative leader. In opposition, he took up his fight against Harold Wilson and so began a raillery reminiscent of Pitt and Fox or Disraeli and Gladstone more than a century before. Then in June 1970, when Wilson went to the country expecting to win without a shadow of doubt, the Tories ousted the Labour

Party and Edward Heath became prime minister.

He formed his administration of able, competent men, but he tried to go it alone. Still he was determined to take Britain into the European Economic Community, and succeeded in doing so in January 1973. Not everybody was delighted with his achievement and when he went to Brussels to seal Britain's entry, a woman threw a bottle of ink over him.

His downfall came through the unions who objected to his Industrial Relations Act which he had pushed through Parliament, and his confrontation with the striking miners towards the end of 1973. Heath imposed a three-day week for industry, and the country was split down the middle in its opinion of the confrontation. Heath, confident that the majority were in favour of him, took the issue to the polling booths in February 1974. Heath lost his gamble, and Labour gained five more seats than the Tories. Much of the Tory vote was lost to the Liberals, but they refused to support the Conservatives, and a week later, Heath conceded defeat and resigned in favour of Harold Wilson.

Heath continued to lead the opposition until February of the following year, 1975, when he was toppled from the Tory Party leadership by Mrs Margaret Thatcher, the first woman to become leader of a British political party. Heath refused to serve under Mrs Thatcher in the Shadow Cabinet and retired to the back benches.

Heath, who was Britain's fourth batchelor prime minister, made it to the top from very humble beginnings. From early childhood he was encouraged by a doting mother, who idolised him, but did not live long enough to share his ultimate success. Apart from being a successful politician, he is also an accomplished musician, his main instrument being the organ, and a successful yachtsman.

Leonard James Callaghan

Born 27 March 1912
Married Audrey Moulton (1
son, 2 daughters)
Ministry 1976– 79 (Labour) –
Queen Elizabeth II

When Harold Wilson announced his resignation to a surprised House of Commons, and an equally surprised nation, on 16 March 1976, James Callaghan threw himself into the leadership battle with a fierce determination to win. He achieved success three weeks later at the end of a three-round contest in which the five other Cabinet minister contestants were eliminated, and accepted the premiership on 5 April. As the battle for the premiership was being fought, so was the battle for the Football League championship, and when Callaghan emerged triumphantly from the fray with 176 votes (a majority of 39 over Michael Foot, his only remaining opponent), his nine-year-old grandson proudly told his father: 'Do you know granddad's got more points than Arsenal has!'

The deeply divided Labour Party had been held together for twenty-three years by Harold Wilson and it was generally agreed that the only one who could continue to hold it together was Callaghan, with his moderate stance, and his wide parliamentary experience. His first words to his party were: 'I want no cliques. There will be no insiders and no outsiders. So far as the past is concerned, I shall wipe the slate clean and ask everyone else to do the same—and that includes members of the self-appointed groups.' This latter referred to the Tribune group on the left of the party, and the Manifesto group on the right. He continued: 'None of you holds the Ark of the Covenant. The party workers in the country expect your first loyalty to be not to your group meetings but to the Labour Party meetings.'

James Callaghan firmly believes in loyalty—to his party, to his country, to his family, and to his Baptist faith. His climb to the top from humble beginnings has been through his steadfastness. His father, James Callaghan, a seaman on the Royal Yacht, died when James was nine years old, leaving the family penniless. But, despite their financial hardship, Charlotte Callaghan taught her son and his elder sister Dorothy, the real values of life.

When he left Portsmouth Northern Grammar School at the age of 17, James Callaghan became a clerk in the Inland Revenue. 'After her experience as a widow, my mother had only one idea—to get me into an absolutely safe job that guaranteed a pension at sixty. And can you blame her?' he said. But after seven years Callaghan left the dull clerk's job to become assistant secretary of the Inland Revenue Staff Federation. It was in this job that he met Harold Laski, the Labour Party intellectual giant, who was looking for Labour MPs, and who recognised and encouraged Callaghan's potential for politics.

Then came World War II and in 1942 Callaghan joined the Navy and was posted to the Admiralty in London, on the staff of the Director of Naval Intelligence. Meantime, Laski was still intent on getting Callaghan into politics, and in 1943 proposed him as prospective candidate to the selection committee at Reading. Callaghan was rejected in favour of Ian Mikardo, but a year later he was put up for selection at Cardiff South, and this time was successful—defeating his rival George Thomas by one vote. However, the jubilant Callaghan had no time to become acquainted with the constituency he hoped to represent for he was posted to Ceylon and was still there when the war ended and Churchill was preparing for a general election. Callaghan was flown home three weeks before polling day and, in the election of 5 July 1945, Lieutenant L. J. Callaghan polled a 5,944 majority over his Conservative rival, Sir Arthur Evans, who had held the seat for twenty-one years.

Callaghan took his seat in the Commons at the age of thirty-two, and two years later became parliamentary secretary at the Ministry of Transport, where he was responsible for the safety measures of cats' eyes and zebra crossings on British roads. It peeved him that he was never given credit for these major innovations.

In 1951 the Conservatives regained power and Callaghan joined the Shadow Cabinet as spokesman on colonial affairs. In Harold Wilson's government of 1964 he became Chancellor of the Exchequer and, for three years, fought desperately to avoid devaluing the pound. However, in 1967 he was forced to devalue by 14.3 per cent; he resigned as Chancellor and became Home Secretary.

In 1970 he was in opposition to Edward Heath's Conservative Government and became Foreign Secretary in 1974 with Labour's re-election. By now he had held the three major posts in the Cabinet and was one of the most experienced politicians in the Labour Party, fitting him very well to succeed Harold Wilson as leader of the Party and prime minister—which he did on 5 April 1976.

Wilson's legacy to Callaghan was not a happy one, with unemployment reaching over 1.25 million and an inflation rate of about 15 per cent. Moreover, public morale and Britain's prestige abroad were low, and the unions were becoming restless over the high unemployment figures and the government's pay policy. Callaghan was faced with a difficult task to keep the Labour Party as what they have become to consider themselves, 'the natural ruling party'. Only history will show how he fared.

Callaghan, a dedicated politician, has been helped to the top by his wife, Audrey, whom he married in 1938. Their marriage is a happy one and Callaghan admits that he would be lost without his wife, whom he met when they were both teenage Baptist Sunday School teachers. An affable, likeable man, he shuns social functions, and when he is not attending Parliament he relaxes on his 138 acre farm at Ringmer in Sussex.

Glossary of Historical Events

1 SOUTH SEA BUBBLE The South Sea Company was a stock-jobbing scheme devised in 1711 to meet a financial crisis in Britain, brought about by the Whig financiers refusing to lend money to the Tory Government. The company took over the national debt in exchange for a trading monopoly in the South Seas and South America. But Spain would not allow the company to trade, so they speculated the money in other ways and, by clever rigging of the market, £100 shares were inflated to over £1000. People from all walks of life invested their money in the hope of making a quick fortune—and some did. Then in 1721 the bubble burst, causing England's first great stockmarket panic, and thousands of people were ruined.

2 SINKING FUND A fund built up from revenue set aside to accumulate at interest and used to pay off a debt.

3 10 DOWNING STREET The official London residence of the British prime minister. This was offered by King George II to Sir Robert Walpole, Britain's first prime minister, as a present in 1738. Walpole, although corrupt in other ways, never accepted gifts or money from George II, and declined it as a personal gift, but accepted it as an official residence for the holder of the premiership.

4 WAR OF JENKINS' EAR A war (1739–41) between Britain and Spain brought about by the Spanish coastguards at Havana allegedly cutting off the ear of Robert Jenkins, a British merchant, after they had pillaged his ship in an effort to prevent him illegally trading in Spanish America. Jenkins carried his ear in a jar to the House of Commons, where MPs, in their anger, forced Walpole to declare war on Spain. France supported Spain and this war merged into the War of the Austrian Succession.

5 BOY PATRIOTS A group of ambitious and high-minded young protestant Whigs, led by Lord Cobham of Stowe, one of Marlborough's generals. They were jealous of Britain's good name, contemptuous of Hanover and against all corruption. They called themselves 'patriots'; Walpole, whom they eventually brought down, scornfully called them 'boys'. George Grenville and the Elder Pitt were among the group.

6 WAR OF THE AUSTRIAN SUCCESSION A war (1740–8) in Europe over the succession to the Habsburg Empire, following the death of the Emperor Charles VI. The Emperor, who had no male heirs, had settled the empire on his daughter, Maria Theresa, by pragmatic sanction. Frederick the Great of Prussia, ignoring the sanction, invaded Silesia. France joined with Spain, Bavaria and Saxony against Austria. Britain and Holland supported Austria. The war was settled in 1748 by the Treaty of Aix-la-Chapelle. France and Britain restored their conquests to Austria, but Prussia kept Silesia.

7 SEVEN YEARS' WAR A war (1756–63) between Frederick the Great of Prussia (supported financially and militarily by Britain), and Austria, France and Russia, fought in North America, India and Europe.

8 TREATY OF PARIS A treaty (1763) ending the Seven Years' War. Britain gained Canada, all French territory east of the Mississippi, Breton Island, Florida and control of India. Cuba was given to Spain. Among France's gains were Guadeloupe and Martinique. The Elder Pitt, who had directed the war, felt betrayed by the treaty's distribution of territory.

9 BOSTON TEA-PARTY The dumping into Boston Harbour of three shiploads (342 chests) of tea by colonists protesting against British taxation on tea. The fight against taxation led to the War of American Independence.

10 ROYAL MARRIAGE ACT An act passed in 1772 by which English descendants of George II must obtain Royal consent to marry if they are under twenty-five, or give twelve months' notice of their intention to the Privy Council if over twenty-five.

11   CATHOLIC EMANCIPATION   Granting to Catholics the right to vote and to sit in Parliament. Before the Catholic Emancipation Act (1829) a Catholic was not allowed to vote, become an MP, or hold public offiice.

12   EAST INDIA COMPANY   A company of merchants, chartered by parliament in 1600, to trade with the East Indies. It was driven out of the East Indies by the Dutch in 1623 and concentrated on trade with India, where Clive's victories over the French enabled it to assume political and economic responsibility of British territories. After the Indian Mutiny (1857) responsibility passed to the Crown (1858) and the company was dissolved in 1874.

13   PETERLOO MASSACRE   An incident on 16 August 1819 when the magistrates ordered the cavalry to charge a crowd of 80,000 industrial workers in St Peter's Fields, Manchester, peacefully petitioning for parliamentary reform and abolition of the corn laws. Eleven people were killed and hundreds injured. Denying the demonstration was peaceful, the magistrates claimed self-defence for the charge. Although the Cabinet privately abhorred their action, for the sake of law and order, they publicly commended it, and introduced the Six Acts to counter revolution.

14   SIX ACTS   Six acts of Parliament passed in December 1819 in order to subdue the working classes after the Peterloo Massacre. These (1) allowed immediate trial for 'cases of misdemeanour'; (2) increased penalties for seditious libel; (3) imposed newspaper stamp duty on magazines containing news; (4) curtailed public meetings; (5) prohibited training in the use of arms; (6) empowered magistrates to search for and seize arms dangerous to public peace.

15   STORMING OF THE BASTILLE   The beginning of the French Revolution when a Paris mob stormed the Bastille (the state prison) on 14 July 1789 as a symbol of the end of absolute royal power.

16   HOLY ALLIANCE   A pact made on 26 September 1815 between Austria, Prussia and Russia by which they agreed to

govern by Christian principles to preserve peace and justice in Europe. It was joined by all European countries except Britain, Turkey and the Vatican.

17 MAHRATTAS   People of West Central India who founded an empire in 1674 after the fall of the Mogul Empire. This degenerated into a confederacy of warring states which were subdued by the British.

18 REFORM BILL   A Bill to enlarge the franchise and reduce inequalities in representation. The first of these (1832) disenfranchised rotten boroughs (small boroughs with few inhabitants) giving fairer representation to large towns and increasing the county and borough franchise. The second Bill (1867) gave the vote to industrial workers, and the Franchise Bill (1884) extended the vote to most men over the age of twenty-one. In 1918, suffrage was extended to all men over twenty-one and women over thirty, in 1928 to women over twenty-one and in 1969 to both men and women over eighteen.

19 CORN LAWS   Various laws, passed between 1436 and 1842, regulating the corn trade. The most controversial were those of the nineteenth century, especially that of 1815 which imposed high duty on imported corn, thus keeping up the prices of British corn. Hardship among the poor, caused by the laws, led to riots and in 1839 an Anti-Corn Law League was formed to force the government to repeal them. After much suffering and great political storms, the laws were repealed by Robert Peel on 25 June 1846.

20 TOLPUDDLE MARTYRS   A group of six farmworkers in Tolpuddle, Dorset, sentenced to seven years transportation for forming a trade union.

21 PROTECTIONISTS   Those in favour of protecting the home market by imposing import tariffs on foreign goods.

22 CONSPIRACY TO MURDER   A bill designed to tighten up the conspiracy law, introduced by Lord Palmerston in 1858 in response to French demands for measures to be taken against 'this nest of assassins' after the Italian, Felice Orsini, had hurled

146

a bomb at Napoleon III. The bomb and the assassination plot had been made in England.

23 INDIAN MUTINY A rebellion (1857–8) of Bengal sepoys against British rule in India, caused by Hindu opposition to British social reforms. It resulted in the India Act by which rule of India passed to the Crown from the East India Company.

24 PLIMSOLL LINE A set of lines on a ship indicating the depth to which the ship may be safely loaded in varying waters and conditions. Named after Samuel Plimsoll, the reformer who fought for it.

25 PRIMROSE DAY The day, 19 April, on which flags were sold in the streets in aid of the Primrose League, an association for Conservative propaganda formed in 1883 in memory of Lord Beaconsfield (Disraeli).

26 SCORCHED-EARTH POLICY An episode during the Boer War when British forces burned the crops and homes of the Boer farmers and imprisoned the women and children in concentration camps.

27 CARLTON CLUB England's chief Conservative club, in Pall Mall, London, founded in 1831 by the Duke of Wellington and his political associates.

28 SIEGE OF SIDNEY STREET A siege in Sidney Street, Stepney on 3 January 1911. Three anarchists, led by a Russian nicknamed 'Peter the Painter' barricaded themselves in a house after having robbed a jewellers in Houndsditch and shot dead three policemen. When police and firemen failed to smoke them out, soldiers were brought in from the Tower of London to shoot them out. Two of them were found charred to death, but 'Peter the Painter' somehow managed to escape and was never seen again.

29 DARDANELLES CAMPAIGN A campaign advocated by Churchill during World War I in which allied troops landed in Gallipoli on 25 April 1915 with the intention of storming the Dardanelles and opening up a supply route to Russia which had

been cut off after Turkey had entered the war. The campaign was a complete failure and more than 8,000 troops were killed and thousands more wounded.

30 LEAGUE OF NATIONS An association of 62 independent states formed on 16 January 1920 with the object of preserving international peace and security. It was not a very successful organisation and in April 1946 it was dissolved and re-emerged as the United Nations.

31 ZINOVIEV LETTER A letter, said to be from Gregory Zinoviev, leader of the Russian Communists, to the British Communist Party, advocating preparation for armed revolution. The Foreign Office, after protesting to the Soviet government, issued the text of the letter to the newspapers just before the general election.

32 SUEZ CRISIS An incident in 1956 when President Nasser nationalised the Suez Canal on 26 July in order to raise money for the Aswam high dam after Britain and the US withdrew their offers of financial aid. Efforts to negotiate a settlement with Nasser failed and resulted in an invasion of Egypt by Israel on 29 October and British and French bombardment of Cairo and the canal area on 31 October. On 6 November Russia threatened to intervene on the side of Nasser, and the US ordered a global alert of her armed forces. War seemed imminent, then the British Government agreed to a ceasefire.

Chronological List of Prime Ministers

Administration

George I (1714–27)
1721	Sir Robert Walpole	Whig

George II (1727–60)
1742	Spencer Compton	Whig
1743	Henry Pelham	Whig
1754 (1)	Duke of Newcastle	Whig
1756	Duke of Devonshire	Whig
1757 (2)	Duke of Newcastle	Whig

George III (1760–1820)
1762	Earl of Bute	Tory
1763	George Grenville	Whig
1765 (1)	Marquis of Rockingham	Whig
1766	William Pitt (the Elder)	Whig
1767	Duke of Grafton	Whig
1770	Lord North	Tory
1782 (2)	Marquis of Rockingham	Whig
1782	Earl of Shelburne	Whig
1783 (1)	Duke of Portland	Coalition
1783 (1)	William Pitt (the Younger)	Tory
1801	Henry Addington	Tory
1804 (2)	William Pitt (the Younger)	Tory
1806	Lord Grenville	Whig
1807 (2)	Duke of Portland	Tory
1809	Spencer Perceval	Tory
1812	Lord Liverpool	Tory

George IV (1820–30)
1827	George Canning	Tory
1827	Lord Goderich	Tory
1828	Duke of Wellington	Tory

William IV (1830–7)
1830	Earl Grey	Whig

1834	(1)	Lord Melbourne	Whig
1834	(1)	Sir Robert Peel	Tory
1835	(2)	Lord Melbourne	Whig

Victoria (1837–1901)

1841	(2)	Sir Robert Peel	Tory
1846	(1)	Lord John Russell	Whig
1852	(1)	Earl of Derby	Conservative
1852		Earl of Aberdeen	Coalition
1855	(1)	Viscount Palmerston	Liberal
1858	(2)	Earl of Derby	Conservative
1859	(2)	Viscount Palmerston	Liberal
1865	(2)	Earl (Lord John) Russell	Liberal
1866	(3)	Earl of Derby	Conservative
1868	(1)	Benjamin Disraeli	Conservative
1868	(1)	William Ewart Gladstone	Liberal
1874	(2)	Benjamin Disraeli	Conservative
1880	(2)	William Ewart Gladstone	Liberal
1885	(1)	Marquis of Salisbury	Conservative
1886	(3)	William Ewart Gladstone	Liberal
1886	(2)	Marquis of Salisbury	Conservative
1892	(4)	William Ewart Gladstone	Liberal
1894		Earl of Rosebery	Liberal
1895	(3)	Marquis of Salisbury	Conservative

Edward VII (1901–10)

1902		Arthur James Balfour	Conservative
1905		Sir Henry Campbell-Bannerman	Liberal
1908		Henry Herbert Asquith	Liberal (coalition 1915)

George V (1910–36)

1916		David Lloyd George	Coalition
1922		Andrew Bonar Law	Conservative
1923	(1)	Stanley Baldwin	Conservative
1924	(1)	James Ramsay MacDonald	Labour
1924	(2)	Stanley Baldwin	Conservative
1929	(2)	James Ramsay MacDonald	Labour (National 1931)
1935	(3)	Stanley Baldwin	National

Edward VIII (1936)
George VI (1936–52)

1937	Arthur Neville Chamberlain	National
1940 (1)	Sir Winston Churchill	Conservative (coalition 1945)
1945	Clement Attlee	Labour
1951 (2)	Sir Winston Churchill	Conservative

Elizabeth II (1952–)

1955	Sir Anthony Eden	Conservative
1957	Harold Macmillan	Conservative
1963	Sir Alec Douglas-Home	Conservative
1964 (1)	Sir Harold Wilson	Labour
1970	Edward Heath	Conservative
1974 (2)	Sir Harold Wilson	Labour
1976	James Callaghan	Labour

Index

153

156

157